Contents

Foreword

Dining culture is an art that draws people together and fosters harmony. A nation's cuisine is without doubt one of the most important values of any developed civilization, and familiarity with "foreign food" contributes—perhaps even more than we realize—to increased tolerance and mutual understanding between different cultures.

The sixteenth-century French poet Rabelais was well aware of this as he wrote in his novel *Pantagruel*, "Every rational human being who builds a house starts with the kitchen...." And before setting off for the Congress of Vienna in 1815, the French foreign minister Talleyrand reminded his king, Louis XVIII, "Sire, I need pots far more than instructions...."

Thus it is a special pleasure to introduce the *Délices de France* series, a collaborative effort involving many of the preeminent chefs working in France today. Almost 100 masters of their trade are gathered in these comprehensive collections of recipes, representing various geographical regions and branches of the culinary arts that have made French cuisine so renowned: bakers and pastry chefs, chocolatiers, sommeliers, and many more.

All the contributors have already made a name for themselves, or are well on their way to doing so. With its wealth of practical details and background information, *Délices de France* will appeal to anyone with culinary interests—from the hobby cook looking to impress guests at a dinner party to the experienced gourmet interested in improving their craft.

Roger Roucou
1988 President of the *Maîtres Cuisiniers de France*

DÉLICES DE FRANCE

DESSERTS

DINE WITH FRANCE'S MASTER CHEFS

KÖNEMANN

Acknowledgements

We would like to thank the following people and businesses for their valuable contributions to this project:

Baccarat, Paris; Champagne Veuve Clicquot Ponsardin, Reims; Cristallerie de Hartzviller, Hartzviller; Cristallerie Haute-Bretagne, Paris; Établissements Depincé Laiteries Mont-Saint-Michel, Saint-Brice; FCR Porcelaine Daniel Hechter, Paris; Harraca/Roehl Design, Paris; La Verrerie Durobor, Soigny (Belgium); Le Creuset Fonte Émaillée, Fresnoy-le-Grand; Renoleau, Angoulême; Maison Mossler Orfèvre Fabricant, Paris; Manridal, Wasselonne; Moulinex, Bagnolet; Pavillon Christofle, Paris; Porcelaine Lafarge-Limoges, Limoges; Porcelaines Bernardaud, Limoges; Porcelaines de Sologne et Créations Cacharel, Lamotte-Beuvron; Porcelaines Raynaud, Limoges; Rémy & Associés Distribution France, Levallois-Perret; Robert Havilland et C. Parlon, Paris; SCOF, St-Rémy-sur-Durolle; Tupperware, Rueil-Malmaison; Villeroy & Boch, Garges-lès-Gonesse; Zanussi CLV Système, Torcy.

Level of difficulty of the recipes:

★   easy

★★   advanced

★★★   challenging

© 1997 Original edition: Fabien Bellahsen, André Delmoral, Daniel Rouche
Original titel: Délices de France, Desserts Froids, Chauds et Glacé
Photographs: Michel Tessier
Wine recommendations: Georges Ciret
(Member of the Association of Professional Sommeliers)

© 1999 for the English edition
Könemann Verlagsgesellschaft mbH
Bonner Straße 126, D-50968 Köln

Translation from French: Jane Carroll
English-language editor: Sally Schreiber
Coordination and typesetting: Agents – Producers – Editors, Overath
Reproduction: Reproservice Werner Pees
Production manager: Detlev Schaper
Printing and binding: Leefung Asco Printers, Hong Kong

Printed in China

ISBN 3-8290-2746-X

10 9 8 7 6 5 4 3 2 1

Chefs' Foreword

For perhaps the first time in history, the *Délices de France* series has gathered the recipes of a large number of well-known chefs in a comprehensive collection of the delicacies of French cuisine. French cooking is revered throughout the world, and we believe that this portion of our cultural heritage, which so greatly enhances the joy and pleasures of life, is one of which we can be proud.

The cookbooks in this series offer a broad panorama of carefully selected culinary delights, and seek to build a bridge between experts from the various gastronomic professions and all friends of fine dining. It gives us, the chefs, the possibility to set down our expertise in writing and to disseminate our professional secrets, thus enriching and furthering the Art of Cooking. Once a luxury, *haute cuisine* is no longer limited to the patrons of elegant restaurants. The recipes presented here range in difficulty from straightforward to quite complex, and are intended to offer you ideas and encouragement in the preparation of your daily meals.

Allow yourself to be inspired! In this collection you will find novelties, acquaint yourself with regional and exotic specialties, and rediscover old favorites. There is a strong continuity between these recipes and the great tradition of French cooking—a rich and varied table offering a broad palette of gourmet pleasures ranging from the simple and light to the extravagant. We have dedicated our lives to this cuisine and are delighted to invite you on this voyage of culinary exploration.

We have made the details in the recipes as clear as possible in order to make it easier to try them at home. In this process, we illustrate our art, which provides a treat both for the palate and for the eye—two pleasures that go hand-in-hand in cooking. With a little practice, you will soon be skilled enough to turn the everyday into the extraordinary, and to impress your guests with culinary masterpieces.

In a special way, the Art of Cooking fosters the social, interpersonal side of life: It is no coincidence that food accompanies all the important milestones of our lives, from a family sitting down together at the table, to holiday celebrations and weddings, to business deals and political meetings.

We are pleased to present you with our most successful creations, so that you can share their pleasures with your loved ones. And we hope that you will have as much fun trying out these recipes as we did creating them.

Furthermore, we hope that the culinary specialties presented in *Délices de France* may serve as an ambassador throughout the world for the enjoyment and pleasures of life, and that this book may in some way contribute both to mutual understanding among cultures and to the refinement of culinary delights.

Good luck in trying out the recipes!
From the chefs of *Délices de France*

Beer

Ingredients:

- 10½ oz/300 g sablée pastry (see basic recipe)
- ¾ cup plus 1 tbsp/200 g light brown sugar
- 2 tbsp butter
- 2 eggs
- ⅔ cup/150 ml light beer

Serves 6
Preparation time: 10 minutes
Cooking time: 30 minutes
Difficulty: ✳

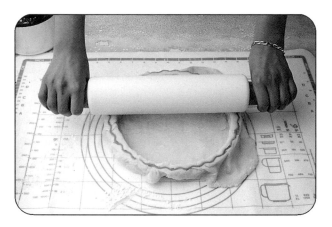

1. Carefully roll out the pastry.

You might already know beer as an ingredient of soup and court-bouillon, or as a wash for the rind of strong cheeses such as Maroilles. You have probably used beer yourself when making a very light crêpe batter. But a beer tart? It sounds unlikely, but try it, and be pleasantly surprised!

This is an attractive dessert, quick and easy to make, and ideal for serving at an informal buffet supper.

Use a light, pale beer, and brown sugar, which our chef recommends because it dissolves more slowly than white sugar, producing a beautifully caramelized layer at the bottom of the tart.

Bake the tart slowly in a moderate oven, checking occasionally to see that it does not brown too much. Serve it warm, and finish it to the last crumb, because it cannot be reheated and does not keep well.

A good beer might seem to be the right choice to accompany the tart. However, our wine expert points out that brandy goes particularly well with desserts; he suggests a marc, or simply a good coffee.

2. Line a shallow pie plate or tart form with the pastry; prick the bottom of the pastry lightly with a fork.

3. Spread the sugar evenly over the pastry bottom.

4. Cut the butter into strips and distribute these evenly over the sugar.

Tart

5. Break the eggs into a bowl and whisk briskly. Add the beer and beat again.

6. Pour this mixture over the sugar and butter; bake the tart for 30 minutes in a moderate oven. Serve warm, hot or cold.

Frangipane

1. Pour the sifted flour and the sugar into a bowl. Reserving a little of the beaten eggs for brushing the top of the gâteau, add the rest to the flour and sugar and blend together.

Ingredients:
- ¾ cup plus 1 tbsp/100 g flour, sifted
- ¾ cup confectioner's sugar
- 5 eggs, lightly beaten
- 2 cups/500 ml milk
- 4½ tbsp/50 g ground sweet almonds
- 3½ tbsp/50 g butter, softened
- vanilla extract
- bitter almond extract
- 14 oz/400 g puff pastry (see basic recipe)
- ⅓ cup/50 g confectioners' sugar

Serves 6
Preparation time: 10 minutes
Cooking time: 30 minutes
Difficulty: ✷

2. Pour in the milk, stirring continuously.

Frangipane, also called *frangipani*, owes its name to an Italian nobleman who lived in Paris in the 16th century and invented a perfume based on bitter almonds. The novel perfume gave French confectioners the idea of making a delicious cream with the almonds. In this recipe, a few drops of almond extract are necessary to release the full flavor of the ground almonds.

Make the puff pastry with butter, but keep it as light as possible because the frangipane is already very rich. Bake until the pastry is golden brown.

This Frangipane Pie, like other desserts based on almonds or honey, is typical of the culinary delights of the Languedoc. In some regions of France, frangipane becomes a filling for *Galettes des Rois*, pastries traditionally eaten on Twelfth Night, or Epiphany. Enjoy this delicious treat in the company of friends at the end of your Christmas and New Year festivities!

According to our wine expert, a Sauternes goes marvelously with the flavor of almonds, and he warmly recommends a Château Coutet Barsac.

3. Add the ground almonds and softened butter, and beat the mixture vigorously to a paste. Stir in the vanilla and almond extracts.

4. Roll out half of the puff pastry and line a tart form with it. Prick the bottom of the shell lightly with a fork. Cut off the excess pastry and pinch the edges lightly.

Pie

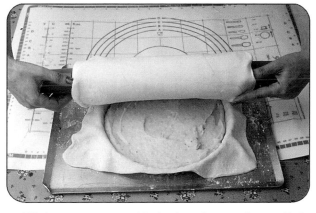

5. Fill the pastry case with the frangipane mixture. Roll out the remaining pastry and cover the tart, pinching the edges together.

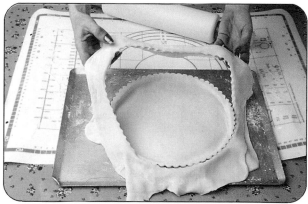

6. Brush the top with the reserved egg, and bake for about 30 minutes in a moderate oven. Immediately before serving, sprinkle with confectioners' sugar. This dessert is best eaten warm.

Raspberry

Ingredients:
2 cups/500 ml milk
1 vanilla bean
5 eggs, separated
$\frac{1}{2}$ cup plus 2 tbsp/ 150 g superfine sugar
4 leaves gelatin
1 cup/250 ml heavy cream
14 oz/400 g raspberries
16 ladyfingers

Serves 6
Preparation time: 40 minutes
Cooking time: 10 minutes
Chilling time: 4 hours
Difficulty: ✶ ✶

1. Add the vanilla bean to the milk and bring to a boil; remove the bean. In a separate bowl, beat the sugar and egg yolks. Slowly pour the milk into the yolks and sugar, whisking briskly. Cook as for a crème anglaise (see basic recipe).

The origins of this well-known dessert are obscure, but it is similar to an English dessert, which may have been named in honor of the wife of King George III in the late 18th century. At one time it appeared only on the menus of expensive hotels but now, although still highly regarded by gourmets, it has become a popular family dessert in France.

The basis of this cold dessert is a custard cream, often with fruit, placed in a mold lined with ladyfingers or other cake.

When pouring the hot milk into the egg yolks, remember to keep beating vigorously; otherwise the yolks will cook and the mixture will become lumpy.

The chantilly, on the other hand, needs the opposite treatment: Use a wooden spatula, rather than a whisk, and fold it into the custard as lightly as possible so that it does not collapse or liquefy.

Crowned with cream and studded with raspberries, Raspberry Charlotte looks very attractive, and makes a royally elegant end to a meal.

Champagne is called for here: Veuve Clicquot, of course!

2. Mix the gelatin with a little water. Stir it into the custard while it is still hot, and allow to cool. Line a charlotte mold with the ladyfingers.

3. Whip the chilled heavy cream to make a chantilly (see basic recipe) and chill.

4. When the custard has cooled and begun to thicken, gently fold in ¾ of the crème chantilly. Add sugar to the rest of the cream and return to refrigerator.

Charlotte

5. Fill the lined mold ⅓ full with the custard and cream mixture, chill, and cover with a layer of raspberries. Repeat this step until the form is filled, ending with a layer of custard.

6. Chill for 2 or 3 hours. Just before serving, turn out the charlotte onto a plate. Decorate with the sweetened chantilly cream and a few raspberries. Serve with a raspberry coulis, if desired (see basic recipe).

Soufflé

1. For the Polignac almonds, make a syrup of the superfine sugar and ¾ cup/200 ml water. Add the almonds and stir briefly over the heat. Drain them, place on a baking sheet, then toast under the grill, stirring from time to time. Allow to cool.

2. For the pastry cream, whisk the egg yolks while adding the sugar (reserving 1 tbsp) and flour. Place the vanilla bean in the milk and bring to a boil. Pour the hot milk into the eggs, blending to make a pastry cream (see basic recipe).

3. Butter a soufflé dish, sprinkle it with sugar, and chill. Whisk the egg whites into soft peaks, adding the reserved 1 tbsp sugar when they start to stiffen.

Ingredients:
¾ cup plus 1 tbsp/200 g superfine sugar
1 cup/100 g slivered almonds
For the pastry cream:
6 egg yolks
¾ cup plus 2 tbsp/215 g sugar
6½ tbsp/50 g pastry flour
2 cups/500 ml milk
1 vanilla bean
3½ tbsp/50 g butter
10 egg whites
1 small glass of Grand Marnier
confectioners' sugar for decoration

Serves 6
Preparation time: 20 minutes
Cooking time: 20 minutes
Difficulty: ✳ ✳

According to one theory, this soufflé was created in honor of the illustrious Polignac family. In any case, it is an aristocratic dish, the prince of soufflés. It must be served hot, straight out of the oven after it has risen well. Any delay will cause it to collapse.

At one time the name of the dish was spelled *soufflet*, meaning a slap in the face. Could this be why the dish is regarded with a certain amount of trepidation? A beautifully risen soufflé, whether served as appetizer or dessert, is always greeted with gasps of appreciation. For an attractive golden surface, dust the soufflé with a little confectioners' sugar before baking is complete.

Start heating the pastry cream half an hour before serving the soufflé. Add a small amount of the whipped egg whites to the hot cream, vigorously beating all the time, to lighten the mixture. Gently fold in the rest of the egg whites. Make sure you keep stirring the pastry cream while it is cooking so that it does not stick to the bottom of the pan. Afterwards melt a little butter on the surface to prevent a skin forming.

Soufflé Polignac is an exquisite dessert and will guarantee you a cordon-bleu reputation. Our wine expert recommends a good pink champagne to go with it.

4. Stir the Grand Marnier into the pastry cream, heat again, add about ¼ of the egg whites and blend together vigorously. Then lightly fold in the rest of the egg whites.

Polignac

5. Fill ⅓ of the soufflé dish with the pastry cream, and spread with a layer of the Polignac almonds. Repeat. Top with a layer of pastry cream and smooth with a spatula.

6. Clean the rim of the dish with your thumb to help the soufflé rise. Bake for about 12 minutes in a medium-hot oven. A few minutes before the baking is completed, dust the surface with confectioners' sugar, and return the soufflé to the oven until it turns golden brown. Serve immediately.

Pears Poached

Ingredients:
5 fine ripe pears
1 bottle of Chaume
(at least 5 years
old)
1 lemon
¾ cup plus 1 tbsp/
200 g sugar
a sprig of mint

Serves 5
Preparation time: 5 minutes
Cooking time: 20 minutes
Difficulty: *

1. Pour the wine into a pan and bring to a boil.

This is a quick and easy recipes that will be appreciated by busy cooks. Its success depends on the quality of the wine and the pears. Chaume is a white wine from Anjou that requires at least five years of aging to develop its full character and bouquet.

Our chef prefers Conference pears, a winter pear widely grown in the Loire Valley. In summer, you might use William pears. Whatever pears you choose, make sure they are firm, or they will disintegrate while cooking. As soon as you have peeled them, rub them with a slice of lemon to preserve their beautiful white flesh.

Pears Poached in Wine is a stylish and delicious dessert, yet simple to make. For very little effort, you will be generously rewarded by your guests' appreciation. Enjoy the marvelous golden-fruit bouquet of a Quarts de Chaume with this dessert.

2. Peel the pears, but do not remove the stalks.

3. Rub the pears with the halved lemon to help prevent discoloration.

4. Stir the sugar into the wine and simmer gently.

in Wine

5. Add the pears to the pan, cover with a lid, and poach them until just tender.

6. Allow the pears to cool in the syrup. Just before serving, arrange them in a dish and pour the syrup over them. Decorate each pear with a small sprig of mint and serve well-chilled.

Chalande

1. For the brioche dough, mix the yeast with some of the milk. Sift the flour into a bowl; stir in the sugar and salt. Add the eggs, yeast and milk and knead to form a dough. Incorporate the butter and knead thoroughly, then let rise for 2 hours. Butter a shallow tart pan.

2. Stone the prunes; roll out the brioche pastry.

Ingredients:
For the brioche:
½ oz/15 g yeast
⅔ cup/150 ml milk
4 generous cups/
    500 g flour
3½ tbsp/50 g sugar
2 tsp/10 g salt
2 eggs
½ cup/125 g butter,
    softened
For the filling:
1 lb 5 oz/600 g
    prunes
3½ tbsp/50 g apricot
    glaze (see the
    glossary)

Serves 6
Preparation time: 15 minutes
Cooking time: 25 minutes
Difficulty: ✷

This flan is typical of eastern France. It will prove a delightful discovery for those who do not know it—simple to make, quite substantial, and particularly suitable for serving when the wintry weather starts.

A delicious variation can be made with raisins, which are first placed in water which is brought to a boil. Remove them from the heat and allow them to swell for a quarter of an hour. Drain well before spreading on the brioche, that most typically French yeast bread.

There is yet another variation, which children love: Roll out the brioche pastry into a wide strip, and cover the center with apricots. Their weight will press down the middle of the brioche, making the outside edges thicker. Cut into individual portions before placing in the oven.

The Prune and Apricot Flan is a very adaptable dish and a real treat for both children and adults on a cold winter's day.

Our wine expert recommends a prune liqueur.

3. Line the tart pan with the pastry.

4. Prick the bottom of the pastry shell with a fork.

5. Let the pastry rise, then fill with the prunes and bake in a medium oven for 20-30 minutes.

6. Melt the apricot glaze in a little water and spread it over the top of the flan with a pastry brush. Remove the tart from the pan and serve warm or cold.

Charentes

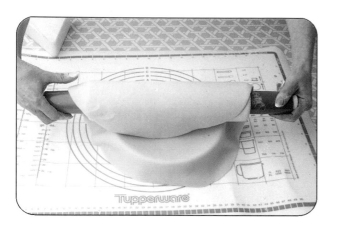

1. *Roll out the sablée pastry and line a cake pan with it.*

Ingredients:
For the pastry case:
8¾ oz/250 g sablée pastry (see basic recipe)
For the filling:
4 eggs
½ cup plus 2 tbsp/ 150 g sugar
1 generous lb/500 g soft white cow's milk cheese
6½ tbsp/50 g flour

Serves 6
Preparation time: 20 minutes
Cooking time: 30 minutes
Difficulty: ✳

2. *Trim the pastry shell and carefully pinch the edges; prick the bottom with a fork.*

As its name suggests, this cheese tart comes from Charentes, where it is made from the local fresh cheese. Given his druthers, our chef prefers to use a Manslois or Ruffec cheese, but any other type of soft white cheese made from cow's milk will do. This recipe is low in calories but high in calcium.

It is important to carry out the various stages of preparation in the right order, and be careful not to over-handle the mixture in the last step or it will collapse. Here is a little trick well known to expert cooks: Add a pinch of salt to the egg whites to prevent them from becoming grainy.

The tart should be brown on top when done. To remove it from the pan, place the tart upside down on a shallow dish until it cools. It can then be easily removed and turned upright onto a serving dish.

This cheesecake can be eaten cold, but on no account put it into the refrigerator: Like all soufflés, it would subside. It can be kept for 48 hours at room temperature.

This sweetish, creamy tart is popular with children—in fact, you'll have to be quick if you want a piece for yourself!

Fruit juice and arabica coffee both go very well with this dessert.

3. *Separate the eggs. Add the sugar to the yolks and whisk together very briskly.*

4. *Beat the egg whites to soft peaks. Add the soft cheese and flour to the egg yolk and sugar mixture and beat together well.*

Cheesecake

5. Add the egg whites to the cheese mixture, folding them in very gently.

6. Fill the tart with the filling and bake 30 minutes in a moderately hot oven. Serve warm or cold.

Pineapple

1. Peel the pineapple carefully, removing the woody eyes. Slice, and remove the core with an apple corer or round pastry cutter.

Ingredients:
6 crêpes (see basic recipe)
For the filling:
1 pineapple
¼ cup/60 g butter
3 tbsp/50 g superfine sugar
½ cup/100 ml creme fraîche
1 cup/250 ml pastry cream (see basic recipe)
⅔ cup/150 ml Grand Marnier

Serves 3
Preparation time: 15 minutes
Cooking time: 10 minutes
Difficulty: ✳

2. Heat the butter and sugar in a frying pan, and gently sauté the pineapple slices until slightly caramelized.

In France, crêpes are traditional fare at the feast of Candlemas and at Mardi Gras. According to tradition, you should make a wish while touching the pan handle before tossing the crêpe. And if you hold a coin very tightly in your left hand while heating your crêpe, you will have wealth for the whole year—but be careful not to let the crêpe fall! For a perfect batter, place the flour, eggs and sugar in a bowl, but don't mix them until you pour in the liquid. If lumps form, strain the mixture through a sieve. The pastry cream should be thick, because it forms the filling for the crêpes. Use a non-stick pan to avoid the need for fat.

The chef recommends bottle-shaped pineapples from the West Indies, but you can of course use canned pineapple. The fresh fruit does not respond well to temperatures below 53 °F/7 °C, so do not store it long in the refrigerator.

Crêpes are ideal for entertaining friends and relations of all ages. Children adore them, but in this case, substitute orange juice for the alcohol.

The golden rule for choosing wine: Serve the same wine, or liqueur, used in preparing the dish. However, our wine expert says you can be a little wild in this case: Offer your guests a glass of rum, which compliments the pineapple beautifully.

3. Whisk the creme fraîche into a chantilly and add to the pastry cream. Pour in half of the Grand Marnier and whisk the mixture vigorously.

4. Spread each crêpe with a spoonful of the mixture and place half a pineapple slice on top.

Crêpes

5. Fold the crêpes and place them on a heat resistant dish. Sprinkle with confectioners' sugar.

6. Warm the plate slightly, pour the rest of the Grand Marnier over the crêpes, flambé them, and serve.

Verveine du Velay

1. *Add the sugar to the egg yolks. Whisk together until pale and foamy.*

Ingredients:
For the crème anglaise:
1 generous cup/ 250 g sugar
8 egg yolks
1½ cup/350 ml milk

¾ cup/200 g heavy cream
6½ tbsp/100 ml Verveine du Velay

Serves 6
Preparation time: 10 minutes
Cooking time: 10 minutes
Chilling time: 2 hours
Difficulty: ✳ ✳

2. *Bring the milk to a boil; then pour it slowly onto the sugar and egg yolks, whisking continuously.*

Verveine du Velay is a spirit that is produced in our chef's home territory. However, he is not in the least chauvinist, and says you may use the liqueur of your choice to blend with the crème anglaise—even fruit juice will do.

Thicken the custard mixture over low heat, stirring continuously to keep it smooth. If lumps appear, however, strain the mixture through a sieve.

As soon as you remove the crème anglaise from the heat, pour it into a bowl standing in cold water to bring the cooking process to an immediate halt. Stir it from time to time while cooling in order to prevent lumps from forming. The whipped cream, like the crème anglaise, must be very cold, otherwise it may liquefy.

This subtle, fresh-tasting dessert will provide a light ending to any meal, whether frugally simple or very grand. It is rich in dairy products and, given its high calcium content, very good for children.

The dessert offers an opportunity to drink a small glass of Verveine du Velay and sample the charm of this liqueur from the Velay region in the Massif Central.

3. *Stir this mixture continuously with a spatula over a very low heat until it thickens, as for a crème anglaise (see basic recipe). Pour into a bowl and allow to cool.*

4. *Whisk the cream into a firm chantilly (see basic recipe), and fold it into the cooled crème anglaise.*

Iced Mousse

5. Stir the Verveine du Velay gently into the mousse.

6. Pour the mixture into a shallow dish and place in the freezer for 1 or 2 hours before serving. Arrange in individual bowls, decorate and serve.

Jaffa

1. *Slice the tops off the oranges. Scoop out the flesh with a spoon, taking care not to pierce the rind.*

Ingredients:
4 Jaffa oranges
4 egg whites
1¼ cups/300 ml
    orange sorbet
1 cup/250 ml pastry
    cream (see basic
    recipe)
3½ tbsp/50 ml Grand
    Marnier
confectioners' sugar

Serves 4
Preparation time: 20 minutes
Cooking time: 6 minutes
Difficulty: ✷ ✷

2. *Beat the egg whites into stiff peaks.*

Our chef has been generous enough to give us this secret recipe, which brought him the prize for the best new dish created in 1979. The name Jaffa in the title refers to those sweet and juicy Israeli oranges that seem to be full of sunshine.

Either buy the sorbet ready-made, or make it with orange juice. Place the filled oranges immediately on ice to prevent the sorbet from melting.

A little trick of the chef to help make smooth pastry cream: Once the cream begins to thicken, remove it from the heat and stir in an additional egg yolk before adding the Grand Marnier.

Mix the stiffly beaten egg whites and the pastry cream with a spatula, using a light, circular movement. To achieve a perfect soufflé, wipe the edge of each orange clean from any pastry cream that has overflowed. Use your finger—it is still the best method! Soufflés cannot be kept waiting, and neither should hungry guests, so serve the dessert as soon as they come out of the oven.

Serving a small glass of well-chilled Cointreau will be a delightful surprise.

3. *Half-fill the oranges with orange sorbet and place them in the freezer.*

4. *Heat the pastry cream while adding the Grand Marnier, and whisk together vigorously.*

Soufflé

5. Just before serving, gently blend the beaten egg whites into the just-warm pastry cream.

6. Fill the oranges with the pastry cream, mounding the mixture slightly above the top edge of the oranges, and bake for 5 or 6 minutes in a hot oven. Decorate with confectioners' sugar and serve.

Iced Grand

Ingredients:
⅔ cup/150 ml heavy cream
1 generous cup/ 250 g sugar
1 cup/250 ml water
6 eggs, separated
⅓ cup/50 g ground praline
6½ tbsp/100 ml Grand Marnier
parchment paper

1. Whisk the cream into a chantilly (see basic recipe) and set aside. Combine the sugar and water and boil gently to make a syrup. Whisk the egg whites until stiff and slowly pour in the syrup, whisking vigorously until cooled (see Italian meringue basic recipe). Set aside.

Serves 6
Preparation time: 45 minutes
Cooking time: 10 minutes
Chilling time: 6 hours
Difficulty: ✳ ✳

A successful soufflé is seen by amateur cooks as the equivalent of a black belt in judo. It is time you tackled one—don't be faint-hearted, our chef will guide you!

Cook the sabayon over a low heat, stirring continuously with a whisk. When finished, it should have doubled in volume and be very frothy.

For the Italian meringue, follow the chef's instructions scrupulously. When the syrup reaches 212 °F/100 °C, start beating the egg whites until they form soft peaks. A pinch of superfine sugar will prevent the egg whites from becoming grainy. By the time the egg whites have formed peaks, the gently boiling syrup will have reached 230 °F/110 °C. Be careful when pouring it onto the egg whites, because it is very hot, and keep whisking continuously to keep the meringue cool. To speed up this operation, you can place the bowl in a dish of iced water.

Above all, do not add the crème chantilly to the meringue until the very last moment. Blend it lightly with a spatula: It must not be over-worked, or the soufflé will collapse.

This recipe gives you plenty of scope for producing a variety of summer desserts if you replace the sabayon with a coulis of fresh fruit. Serve it direct from the freezer, and remember that a soufflé must not be kept waiting: Make sure that your guests are seated and ready for it. And why not serve with it a good Veuve Clicquot brut champagne, which it certainly merits.

2. Add a bit of water to the egg yolks, and beat into a sabayon in a double boiler over a very low heat.

3. When the egg yolks have thickened slightly, add the meringue and blend together.

4. Gently stir the ground praline and the Grand Marnier into this mixture.

Marnier Soufflé

5. When the mixture has cooled, fold in the crème chantilly and blend well.

6. Line a traditional soufflé with parchment paper, making a collar higher than the sides of the dish. Pour in the soufflé mixture to 2 in/5-6 cm above the top of the dish. Place in a freezer for 5 or 6 hours and serve frozen.

1. To make the biscuit, blend the sugar and the eggs over very low heat with an electric mixer. Split the vanilla bean and scrape the pulp into the egg and sugar mixture. Stir in the honey.

Ingredients:
- 6½ tbsp/100 g superfine sugar
- 4 eggs; ½ vanilla bean
- 1 tbsp honey
- 6½ tbsp/50 g flour
- 6½ tbsp/50 g rye flour
- 4½ tbsp/50 g finely ground hazelnuts
- ½ tbsp cornstarch
- 2½ tbsp/25 g ground praline
- 5 tsp/25 g butter
- 3 egg whites
- 3½ tbsp/50 ml sugar syrup
- 3½ tbsp/50 ml hazelnut liqueur
- 2½ oz/75g flaked semi-sweet chocolate

Serves 6
Preparation time: 35 minutes
Cooking time: 20 minutes
Chilling time: 2 hours
Difficulty: ✳ ✳

Our chef created this original recipe for St. Valentine's Day using all locally produced ingredients at the request of the Châteauroux town council. The gâteau has won him various awards, and now he is offering the recipe to you so that you, too, can share the pleasure on a special occasion.

This gâteau is not particularly fragile, but the honey makes it liable to brown to quickly, so keep an eye on the oven while baking. Remember to keep the oven moderate, and all will be well.

The rye flour is optional, but our chef uses it because it combines well with honey. He recommends Acacia honey, which has a particularly strong and pleasant flavor.

If you do not have any ground hazelnuts, use ground almonds instead, and thinly rolled almond paste could be substituted for the chocolate flakes if you like. Blend the praline well with the butter before incorporating them into the meringue. Coarse praline will not properly dissolve in the meringue.

For St. Valentine's Day, or for any occasion when you want to show your affection, the Châteauroux Gâteau will speak volumes.

To complete the pleasurable experience, open a Vouvray Moelleux. This marvelous wine only improves upon better acquaintance.

2. Sift the flours and add them along with the ground hazelnuts and corn starch to the liquid mixture. Blend together well.

3. Place a cake ring on a baking sheet covered with parchment paper. Fill the ring with the hazelnut batter and bake for about 30 minutes in a medium oven.

4. Split the hazelnut biscuit into 3 layers and allow to cool completely. Use the egg whites and sugar syrup to make an Italian meringue (see basic recipe). For the cream filling, mix the ground praline with the butter, then stir gently into the Italian meringue.

Châteauroux

5. Combine the hazelnut liqueur with the corn syrup, and moisten the biscuit layers with the mixture. Using a pastry bag, cover 2 biscuit layers with some of the praline cream, and place one on top of the other. Cover with the remaining biscuit layer.

6. With a spatula, coat the top and sides of the gâteau with the rest of the praline cream, then cover with the chocolate flakes. Chill in the refrigerator for at least 2 hours before serving.

Orange and

1. To prepare the chocolate filling, melt ¾ of the baking chocolate in a double boiler. Heat the crème fraîche, pour the chocolate into it, and whisk vigorously. Add half the Grand Marnier and whisk again until cool.

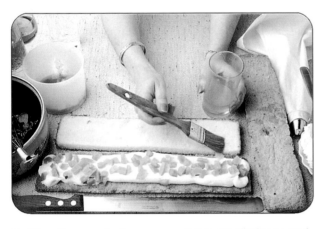

2. Chop the candied orange peel into small pieces and macerate in the remaining Grand Marnier. Slice the génoise into 3 layers. Moisten the bottom layer with a little flavored sugar syrup. Spread with half of the buttercream and sprinkle with candied orange peel.

3. Place a second layer of génoise over the buttercream, and moisten with syrup. With a pastry bag, spread the chocolate filling on this layer, and sprinkle with the rest of the candied orange peel.

Ingredients:
5½ oz/150g semi-sweet
   baking chocolate
½ cup plus 1 tbsp/125 g
   crème fraîche
3½ tbsp/50 ml Grand
   Marnier
1 génoise (see basic
   recipe) baked in a long
   rounded loaf pan
6½ tbsp/100 ml sugar
   syrup flavored with
   Grand Marnier
1¾ cup/450 g
   buttercream (see basic
   recipe)
candied peel of 3
   oranges
1⅓ cups/200 g
   confectioners' sugar

Serves 6
Preparation time: 35 minutes
Cooking time: 5 minutes
Difficulty: ✳ ✳ ✳

Our chef's name for this dessert, *Chèvre à l'orange*, means "orange goat's cheese." He had in mind those *chèvres*, or goat cheeses, of the Touraine and Berry regions that are formed into a cylindrical shape rather like a log.

The candied orange peel should be left in refrigerator to steep in pure Grand Marnier; the longer they are left to macerate the more flavor they will absorb and the better they will be. They will keep up to a year in the refrigerator in a tightly sealed container.

To preserve the shape of the gâteau intact, slice it with a heated knife. For moistening the génoise, undiluted Grand Marnier would be too strong, so mix it with a little unflavored sugar syrup.

Serve this desert slightly chilled: It is particularly delicious in summer.

The recipe has never been published before, and our chef is generously revealing his secret to you. So reserve this very special treat for your nearest and dearest!

Our wine expert suggests offering your guests a Champagne Veuve Cliquot Carte Jaune.

4. Moisten the top layer of the gâteau with the remaining syrup and set it on the chocolate filling.

Chocolate Log

5. Spread the sides of the gâteau with buttercream.

6. Melt the rest of the chocolate in a bain-marie, coat the "log" with it, and carefully dust the cake with confectioners' sugar.

1. For the génoise, beat the sugar and the eggs with an electric mixer with the bowl resting on a slightly warm burner. Mix half of the cocoa with the flour and potato flour, sprinkle onto the egg mixture, combine, and bake 20 minutes in a greased cake pan in a moderate oven.

2. To make the syrup for soaking, heat the sugar syrup and stir in the cocoa and rum. When the chocolate génoise has cooled, slice it into 3 layers. Moisten each with the syrup.

3. To make the mousse, add a few drops of coffee extract to the butter and beat vigorously. Prepare an Italian meringue according to the basic recipe.

Ingredients:
4 eggs; ½ cup/125 g sugar
2½ tbsp bitter cocoa
¾ cup plus 1 tbsp/100 g flour
3½ tbsp/25 g potato flour
5 tbsp/75 g butter
coffee extract
1 ladle Italian meringue
2 tbsp sugared coffee beans
6½ tbsp/100 g chocolate buttercream (see basic recipe)
1½ tbsp bitter cocoa
For the syrup:
6½ tbsp/100 ml sugar syrup
1 tbsp bitter cocoa
3½ tbsp/50 ml white rum

Serves 6
Preparation time: 45 minutes
Cooking time: 20 minutes
Chilling time: 2 hours
Difficulty: ✶ ✶ ✶

This "duet" of a gâteau will definitely strike a pleasurable chord. If you would like to create a "trio" instead of a "duo," you might replace the coffee beans on the first layer with black currants, whose slightly sharp taste goes well with the taste of the coffee mousse, and on the second, spread flakes of chocolate. On the other hand, you could also try a mono version, either all chocolate or all coffee....

Do not allow the butter for the mousse filling to become soft, or the meringue mixture will liquefy. Flavor the butter well with coffee, as the contrast between the tastes of coffee and cocoa gives this gâteau its particular character.

Allow the gâteau to cool thoroughly in the refrigerator before turning it out, to avoid damaging the cake. You can also make it a day in advance, as it will keep perfectly overnight in the refrigerator.

This delightful Duo is always a pleasure, and a good Champagne Veuve Cliquot Grande Dame will only enhance the enjoyment.

4. Stir the butter mixture into the Italian meringue.

Duo

5. Place a layer of chocolate génoise in the bottom of a cake ring. With a pastry bag, spread half of the butter-meringue mixture onto the layer, and scatter a few sugared coffee beans on top.

6. Repeat the process, ending with the third layer of génoise. Place in the refrigerator for 2 hours to become firm. Remove the gâteau from its form, spread the chocolate buttercream smoothly over its sides, and sprinkle the top with the remaining cocoa. Decorate as desired.

Strawberry

1. Add the buttercream to the pastry cream and mix together until thoroughly blended.

Ingredients:
- ¾ cup/200 g buttercream (see basic recipe)
- 2 cups/500 ml pastry cream (see basic recipe)
- 1 rectangular génoise (see basic recipe)
- ⅓ cup/80 ml kirsch
- 1 generous lb/500 g strawberries
- 6½ tbsp/100 g almond paste
- ⅔ cup/100 g confectioners' sugar

Serves 10
Preparation time: 25 minutes
Chilling time: 1 hour
Difficulty: ✳ ✳

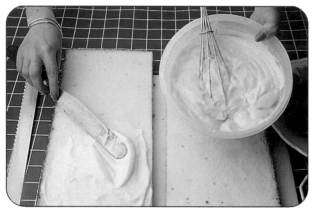

2. Slice the génoise horizontally and moisten the inside of both layers with a little kirsch. Spread ⅓ of the cream mixture on each of the 2 layers.

This delectable strawberry-filled gâteau is sure to delight all those who revel in sumptuous desserts!

Choose a pure kirsch, not one of those fanciful variations that never live up to the promise of their name, to give a delicious flavor to your gâteau. Do be careful not to over-moisten the bottom layer of génoise, however, because it will also be moistened by the cream filling and strawberries.

You might experiment with variations: Raspberries, peaches in syrup, blueberries, bananas poached in a light syrup, or pineapple slices in syrup—whatever takes your fancy. And then think up a suitably whimsical name for your wicked little creation. But do take care to drain the fruit well before arranging it on the pastry cream, otherwise the cake might become soggy.

Strawberry Gâteau is a splendid dessert for a celebration in the summer months when fresh fruit is plentiful.

To drink with it, our wine expert suggests a Champagne Henriot.

3. Arrange the strawberries side by side on one layer.

4. Place the second layer on the first, cream-side down.

Gâteau

5. Spread the remaining cream mixture over the top of the gâteau and place it in the refrigerator for 1 hour to become firm.

6. Roll out the almond paste and cover the top of the gâteau with it. Trim all 4 sides neatly with a knife. Sprinkle confectioners' sugar thickly over the top and serve.

Millefeuille

1. Roll out the puff pastry thinly and cut out 3 circles of about 8 in/20 cm diameter. Prick them lightly with a fork, brush with a little water, and bake in a 430 °F/220 °C oven for about 20 minutes.

Ingredients:
1 lb 5 oz/600 g puff pastry (see basic recipe)
3½ tbsp/50 ml kirsch
1¼ cup/300 ml pastry cream (see basic recipe)
3 tbsp apricot glaze (see glossary)
1⅔ cup/200 g chopped almonds
10½ oz/300 g fondant
4 oz/110 g semi-sweet baking chocolate

Serves 6
Preparation time: 35 minutes
Cooking time: 20 minutes
Chilling time: 1 hour 30 minutes
Difficulty: ✷ ✷ ✷

2. Pour half of the kirsch into the pastry cream and beat vigorously. Spread the cream onto 2 of the cooled pastry circles.

The painter Claude Lorraine, who started out as an apprentice *pâtissier*, or pastry chef, is often said to have been the inventor of puff pastry. However, a certain Feuillet, pâtissier to the Prince de Condé, claimed that it was he who first discovered the effect of pats of butter placed between layers of pastry dough. While the paternity of this happy invention is unlikely to be settled once and for all, this delicious pastry has become a classic.

Before baking the puff pastry, cut it into three squares, trim the corners to form circles, and roll them out. Then refrigerate the circles for 90 minutes or so before baking them. When the three layers of baked puff pastry have cooled, spread the pastry cream between them. Then top with white fondant, while it is hot and runny, and decorate with chocolate. Cover the sides with toasted chopped almonds, and the creation is complete. If you buy ready-made puff pastry, do not fold it before rolling out, or it is likely to become too elastic.

You might wish to add some red fruit in season—for example, strawberries—to give the Millefeuille a lovely fresh taste. Cut the fruit into relatively small pieces and add it to the pastry cream before spreading over the pastry circles. Then finish by dusting with confectioners' sugar.

Our wine expert thinks that for this splendid confection it is well worth uncorking a bottle of Champagne Veuve Clicquot Carte Jaune.

3. Stack the 3 pastry circles so that there are 2 layers of pastry cream filling, and place the Millefeuille on a serving dish.

4. Heat the apricot glaze and spread it over the top and sides of the millefeuille. Toast the chopped almonds under the grill.

5. In a pan, melt the fondant over a low heat, then blend in the rest of the kirsch and a drop of water. At the same time, in another pan, melt the chocolate. Make a cornet out of parchment paper, fill it with the melted chocolate and leave near a source of heat.

6. Pour the fondant over the millefeuille. Quickly draw a spiral pattern on top of the fondant with the point of the cornet. Draw a knife point from the center of the spiral to the rim to form a cobweb pattern. Thickly coat the sides of the millefeuille with the toasted almonds and serve.

Mocha

1. Cut the génoise horizontally into 2 layers. Toast the almonds in the oven and allow to cool.

Ingredients:
1 génoise (see basic recipe)
1 cup/100 g flaked almonds
6½ tbsp/100 ml sugar syrup
3½ tbsp/50 ml white rum
coffee extract
1 cup/250 g coffee-flavored butter-cream (see basic recipe)

Serves 6
Preparation time: 15 minutes
Chilling time: 2 hours
Difficulty: ✳ ✳

2. Mix together a little sugar syrup, the white rum and a drop of coffee extract, and lightly moisten both layers of the génoise with this mixture.

The name "mocha" comes from a Red Sea port in Yemen and refers to a strong and very aromatic variety of Arabica coffee. This Mocha Gâteau probably dates back to the days when coffee-drinking was first introduced in France, and it has since become a highly regarded classic.

Be sparing with the coffee extract because it has a particularly strong taste—a small spoonful will suffice. Use a spatula to cover the gâteau with the buttercream, and a pastry bag with a fluted nozzle to decorate it with rosettes. The top can be dotted with sugared coffee beans, treasures to be picked off by your guests.

This is a dessert that is better eaten the day after it is prepared; if possible, make it in advance. Our chef recommends that it be put in the refrigerator in a well-sealed container at least two hours before serving.

A variation on this recipe uses a praline cream mixed with flaked almonds. The gâteau is then known as a *mascot*, which will certainly bring you good luck.

Whether for a special tea with friends or a children's party, this splendid gâteau will delight everyone's tastebuds. If offered as a dessert, serve with a Champagne Veuve Clicquot rosé: The combination will leave a delicious aftertaste.

3. Cover one layer with half of the coffee buttercream.

4. Place the other layer of génoise on top of the filling.

Gâteau

5. Cover the top and sides of the gâteau with the rest of the coffee buttercream and carefully smooth the surfaces with a spatula.

6. Insert the tips of the flaked almonds into the sides of the gâteau, and decorate according to fancy. Refrigerate for 30 minutes to 2 hours before serving.

Pithiviers

1. To make the filling, combine the ground almonds and confectioners' sugar in a bowl. Work in the butter.

Ingredients:
14 oz/400 g puff pastry
  (see basic recipe)
1 beaten egg
confectioners' sugar
For the filling:
½ cup plus 1 tbsp/100 g
  ground almonds
⅔ cup/100 g
  confectioners' sugar
13 tbsp/200 g butter,
  softened
2 eggs
2 tbsp rum

Serves 8
Preparation time: 20 minutes
Cooking time: 40 minutes
Difficulty: ✶

2. Add the eggs one at a time. Stir until well blended after each addition; then add the rum to the mixture.

This famous pastry dessert is a specialty of the town of Pithiviers near Orléans; but it is traditionally eaten on Epiphany, or Twelfth Nigh, throughout large portions of France. The cook often hides a dried bean or lucky charm in the almond cream to be discovered by one happy guest.

If you use ready-made frozen pastry, our chef recommends that you fold it over a few times to encourage it to rise, as you would if you had made it yourself. Brushing the edges of the bottom layer of pastry with beaten egg helps the two layers stick together. Blend the almond cream using a spatula, and do not add the rum until the last moment.

To give the Pithiviers its traditional appearance, draw a swirling pattern on the top layer of pastry with the point of a knife. But you could also use your imagination to create a fanciful geometric pattern of your own.

Start the baking in a very hot oven to make the pastry rise quickly. After 10 minutes, lower the thermostat to 390°F/200°C. Confectioners' sugar sprinkled on the pastry shortly before it finishes baking will caramelize slightly, giving the Pithiviers its attractive glistening appearance.

This delicious dessert is light and appropriate for all kinds of occasions, but children love it all the more if it conceals the promised surprise.

For the adults, our wine expert suggests a Champagne Veuve Clicquot.

3. Divide the puff pastry in half. Roll it out and cut 2 circles about 12 in/30 cm in diameter. Place one piece of pastry on a baking sheet and brush the outer third of the circle with beaten egg.

4. Place the almond cream mixture in the center of the circle and cover with the second layer of pastry.

5. With a knife, scallop the circumference of the pastry.

6. Glaze the Pithiviers with beaten egg, then draw a swirling pattern on top with a knife. Bake for about 40 minutes in a medium oven. Ten minutes before the end of baking, sprinkle with confectioners' sugar and return to the oven, where it will caramelize slightly.

Raspberry-Filled

1. Melt the chocolate in a pan over very low heat.

Ingredients:
3½ oz/100 g semi-
    sweet baking
    chocolate
⅔ cup/150 ml heavy
    cream
3½ tbsp/50 ml
    raspberry brandy
2 tbsp sugar
8 figs
4½ oz/125 g
    raspberries
parchment paper
mint leaves for
    decoration

Serves 4
Preparation time: 20 minutes
Cooking time: 5 minutes
Difficulty: ✶

2. Cut 8 strips of parchment paper about ⅜ in/1 cm wide. When the chocolate has cooled, spread a little of it over each of the paper strips, using a spatula. Form the strips into semi-circles, place on a flat dish and refrigerate until hardened.

This is a recipe specially created for children. There is nothing difficult about it—just a series of extremely simple steps, so children may even enjoy making these little baskets themselves. In fact, with their small fingers, they will do an excellent job of assembling the pieces.

Pay special attention to selecting the figs, and feel them to make sure are quite ripe.

Melt the chocolate, then allow it to cool. Adding a drop of water will make it easier to handle. Place the chocolate-coated paper strips in the refrigerator so that you have well-hardened handles to place on the figs. The heavy cream should thicken only slightly, and be lightly sweetened with sugar.

Place the little baskets of fresh raspberries on your buffet, as though you had just been picking the fruit in the garden. They add a light-hearted, amusing touch to any party.

To please the children, serve orange juice, full of vitamins. For the grown-ups, however, uncork a Champagne Veuve Cliquot rosé. Its soft pink tinge will beautifully set off these little Raspberry-Filled Fig Baskets.

3. Begin whisking the cream into a chantilly (see basic recipe) while slowly adding the raspberry brandy.

4. Add the sugar to the cream and continue whisking, but stop when the mixture is approximately ¾ of the way to becoming firm. It should still be soft and light.

Fig Baskets

5. With a knife, cut the figs open in a star pattern.

6. Fill the figs with raspberries. Cover a serving dish with the crème chantilly and arrange the figs on it. Gently remove the paper from the chocolate semi-circles, then place one on each fig to form a little basket. Decorate with mint leaves.

Chocolate

1. For the sponge cake, beat the sugar together with the egg yolks until pale. Mix the flour with the cocoa, sift onto the egg yolks and sugar, and blend together.

2. Toast and then crush the hazelnuts. Add half of the nuts together with the melted butter to the egg yolks. Whisk the egg whites to soft peaks, and gently fold them in. Butter and flour a cake pan, pour in the batter, and bake in a moderate oven. Allow to cool.

3. For the filling, heat the light cream. Add the chocolate and stir continuously until it has dissolved.

Ingredients:
For the sponge cake:
6½ tbsp/100 g superfine sugar
6 egg yolks
6½ tbsp/50 g flour
3 tbsp/25 g bitter cocoa
5 egg whites
1 cup/120 g hazelnuts
½ cup/120 g butter, melted
For the filling:
¾ cup/200 g light cream
13 oz/370 g semi-sweet baking chocolate
4½ tbsp/70 g butter
Syrup for moistening:
6½ tbsp/100 ml aged rum
6½ tbsp/100 ml light corn syrup

Serves 6
Preparation time: 35 minutes
Cooking time: 25 minutes
Chilling time: 4 hours
Difficulty: ✶ ✶

The success of this dessert depends mainly on the preparation, so follow our chef's instructions carefully for each step. When making the filling, remove the cream from the heat as soon as it begins to rise in the pan, then add the chocolate and stir until it dissolves. The taste of the filling determines the quality of this gâteau, so choose an extra-fine chocolate. Spread the chocolate filling with a pastry bag, and work quickly, because the chocolate will harden as it cools.

Be sure to dilute the rum with the corn syrup. The sponge cake needs to be well-moistened, and undiluted rum would make it too alcoholic, smothering the other flavors. To make this creation even more special, our chef suggests using milk chocolate and a little coffee extract. Almonds can replace the hazelnuts, if you prefer. And just in case you are still holding back, he guarantees that even a novice cook will have no problems with this recipe.

This dark beauty of a dessert will provide a fitting end to a grand meal—what could be more perfect!

The rich, warm bouquet of a Banyuls Grand Cru will enhance any chocolate dessert.

4. Add the butter to this mixture and whisk vigorously until the consistency is firm.

Hazelnut Truffle

5. Combine the rum and syrup. Slice the sponge cake into 3 layers and moisten each with syrup mixture. Place a layer in a small cake ring. With a pastry bag, cover the sponge cake with a layer of chocolate filling, and sprinkle half of the remaining hazelnuts over it.

6. Repeat the process twice more, smoothing the final layer of filling. Smooth the top and decorate it with a serrated knife. Place in the refrigerator for 4 hours to become firm. Serve the Truffle together with an orange coulis (see basic recipe for raspberry coulis).

Iced Nougat

1. For the nougat, whisk the heavy cream into a chantilly, and prepare the Italian meringue (see the basic recipes).

Ingredients:
For the nougat:
¾ cup/200 g heavy cream
12½ oz/350 g Italian meringue (see basic recipe)
2½ oz/70 g praline
½ cup/100 g candied fruit
For the topping:
2 egg yolks
1 tbsp light cream
1 tsp sugar
For the sauce:
9 tbsp/60 g bitter cocoa
2 cups/500 ml crème anglaise (see basic recipe)
1 mango

Serves 4
Preparation time: 20 minutes
Chilling time: 4 hours
Difficulty: ✳ ✳ ✳

2. Fold the crème chantilly into the Italian meringue. Crush the praline.

You may be familiar with iced nougat—one of those delectable sweets that never go out of fashion. Here our chef strikes a new, sophisticated note to the traditional dessert, and opens up some mouthwatering variations.

The chef recommends adding whipped cream to the meringue, which is rather too sweet on its own, and stirring the cocoa into the crème anglaise while the custard is hot to prevent lumps forming. The crème anglaise should not be allowed to cool, because reheating will harden the egg yolks.

You can slice the mango into attractive shapes with a cookie cutter. Or you might select another kind of tropical fruit—anything that takes your fancy.

Chill the dessert in the freezer for four hours.

Like all frozen desserts, the nougat keeps well, but will you really be able to resist temptation to finish it, with such a luscious sweetmeat in front of you?

Our wine expert suggests that you offer your guests a glass of uniquely-flavored kümmel liqueur or chilled white rum. The combination of flavors is particularly pleasing.

3. Add the candied fruit and crushed praline to the cream and meringue mixture. Blend together gently and set aside.

4. Peel the mango, slice it thinly and place in the refrigerator to chill.

with Mango

5. Fill individual molds, or one large one, with the nougat mixture. Mix the egg yolks with the light cream and sugar. Spread this over each nougat and place in the freezer for 4 hours.

6. Immediately before serving, place the nougat under the broiler for a few seconds to brown. To make the sauce, stir the cocoa into the crème anglaise. Cover the bottom of a serving plate with the sauce, arrange the nougat on it, and serve with the mango slices.

1. For the chocolate cream, melt the chocolate in the crème fraîche over low heat. Add the egg yolk and beat briskly until the mixture is completely cooled.

Ingredients:
3½ oz/100 g semi-sweet baking chocolate
1 tbsp crème fraîche
1 egg yolk
1 cup/250 ml pastry cream; ¾ cup/200 g buttercream (see basic recipes)
3½ tbsp/50 ml syrup
3½ tbsp/50 ml aged rum
6½ tbsp/100 ml passion fruit juice
1 chocolate génoise (see basic recipe)
¾ cup plus 1 tbsp/200 g almond paste (½ cup/ 120 g plain, the rest variously colored)

Serves 6
Preparation time: 30 minutes
Cooking time: 5 minutes
Difficulty: ✶ ✶

2. Prepare a pastry cream as per the basic recipe, but replace the milk with passion fruit juice and add 2 tbsp powdered milk. Add to the buttercream and combine well with an electric mixer. Add half of this mixture to the chocolate and crème fraîche. Blend thoroughly.

Our chef has employed all his skill and imagination in creating this sumptuous dessert. Its smooth ivory coating conceals a rich combination of flavors sure to appeal to the most sophisticated of palates.

The center of the passion flower resembles the traditional symbols of Christ's Passion: A crown of thorns, a hammer and nails. The passion fruit, however, is more likely to be a reminder of summer romances, and even appeared as the "fruit of the loom" design adorning tee-shirts, not so long ago. In fact, the juice of this fleshy yellow South American fruit is aromatic and slightly acidic. It contains few calories but is rich in vitamins A and C.

In the West Indies it is known as the *maracudja*, a name redolent of coconut palms swaying in a tropical breeze.

Our chef suggests grapefruit or orange juice as alternatives in this recipe.

Strike the right note with this exotic dessert: Summon up visions of tropical beaches, and offer your guests a coconut punch or a Champagne Veuve Clicquot Carte Jaune.

3. For the syrup, mix together the corn syrup, rum and passion fruit juice. Slice the génoise into 3 layers and moisten each with the flavored syrup.

4. Spread some chocolate cream mixture on the first layer of génoise.

Diplomat

5. Repeat this process with the second layer, and place it on the first. Top with the third layer of génoise.

6. Spread the remaining chocolate cream over the top and sides of the gâteau. Cover it with a thin layer of plain almond paste, and decorate with a wreath of colored marzipan laurel leaves.

Tropical

Ingredients:
6½ tbsp/100 ml white wine
¾ cup/200 ml water
3 tea bags
1 sprig mint, plus a few extra leaves
3 tbsp/50 g sugar
1 vanilla bean
8¾ oz/250 g bulghur wheat
assortment of seasonal fruit, according to taste

Serves 6
Preparation time: 20 minutes
Cooking time: 5 minutes
Difficulty: ✶

1. Pour the white wine and water into a pan. Add the tea bags, sprig of mint and sugar, and bring to a boil.

Tabbouleh is a Lebanese specialty usually made from bulghur wheat mixed with herbs, tomatoes, onions and mint, and sometimes peppers and lemon. Traditionally it is wrapped in a lettuce leaf and eaten with the fingers.

With this recipe, our chef gives us a sweet, fruit-based version of tabbouleh, rich in delicious, sunny flavors.

There is nothing difficult about preparing this dessert, just make sure that the bulghur wheat is fully softened. The grains cook while absorbing the liquid, which should be close to boiling-hot when poured over the bulghur. Do not hurry the mixing, since each grain must be completely soaked in the liquid.

As for your choice of fruit, make use of different colors. Greens, reds and oranges will combine to produce a visually-delightful conclusion to your meal. Your guests will be dreaming of holidays on palm-fringed beaches....

Our wine expert suggests champagne to go with this dessert.

2. Split the vanilla bean lengthwise, and infuse it in the wine-tea mixture.

3. While still very hot, gradually start pouring the liquid through a sieve onto the bulghur wheat. Mix together thoroughly with a fork. Alternately add the hot liquid and mix until the bulghur wheat has swelled and become tender.

4. Wash and prepare the fruit, and cut the larger fruits into small pieces.

Tabbouleh

5. Gently stir the fruit into the bulghur wheat.

6. Chop the mint leaves finely and add to the tabbouleh. Serve well cooled, accompanied by a traditional crème anglaise (see basic recipe), or one based on passion fruit juice with the addition of powdered milk.

Pear and

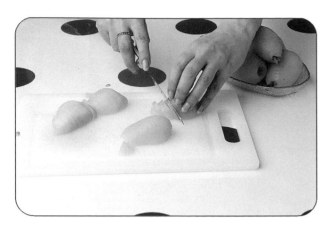

1. Make the sablée pastry according to the basic recipe, but using the ingredients listed above. Slice the pears thinly and drain well.

2. Whisk the eggs and sugar together briskly; stir in the vanilla.

3. Add the crème fraîche and stir vigorously. Roll out the pastry and line the tart pan with it.

Ingredients:

For the sablée pastry:
2 cups/250 g flour
½ cup/125 g butter
2 eggs
4½ tbsp/70 g sugar
For the filling:
16 pear halves in heavy syrup
4 eggs
6½ tbsp/100 g superfine sugar
¼ tsp vanilla
2 cups/500 ml crème fraîche
½ cup/50 g flaked almonds
superfine and confectioners' sugars

Serves 6
Preparation time: 25 minutes
Cooking time: 1 hour
Difficulty: ✳

In French, the words for pear and pastry have in common that they are both used in some expressions referring to people who are rather too easy-going and good-natured for their own good. Here, the combination of pear and pastry makes for one of the most pleasant desserts imaginable.

For the best results, the chef reminds you to make sure that your ingredients are at room temperature—as always when preparing pastries. And to make your tart particularly delicious, she suggests using fresh instead of canned pears. Poach them in water, sugar and vanilla for 30 minutes, or longer if the fruit is very hard.

Perhaps you prefer peaches? Feel free to substitute them instead: they also work wonderfully in this recipe.

The tart can be refrigerated for two to three days without losing any of its flavor.

The entire family will appreciate this tart, and if friends should drop in unexpectedly, you can produce it with a flourish as though you had been keeping it especially for them.

A sparkling sweet cider, well-chilled, goes very nicely with this wonderful tart no matter what time of day you serve it.

4. Arrange the sliced pears on the bottom of the crust and cover with the crème fraîche and egg mixture.

Almond Tart

5. Distribute the flaked almonds over the top.

6. Sprinkle the top of the flan with superfine sugar and bake in a hot oven for 1 hour. Remove from the oven, sprinkle with confectioners' sugar and serve, preferably warm.

Gina's Crêpes

1. For the filling, carefully peel the apple, remove the seeds, and dice. Poach briefly in the cider.

Ingredients:
4 crêpes (see basic recipe)
For the filling:
1 yellow apple
1 glass cider
6½ tbsp/100 ml milk
2 tsp/10 g butter
8 tsp/40 g sugar
3½ tbsp/25 g flour
5 eggs
For the sabayon:
3 eggs
½ cup/125 g superfine sugar
¾ cup/200 ml sweet cider
1 tbsp Calvados

Serves 4
Preparation time: 25 minutes
Cooking time: 25 minutes
Difficulty: ★★

2. Bring the milk to a boil in a saucepan. In a bowl, mix together the butter, sugar and flour, then add to the boiling milk. Whisk vigorously until smooth. Allow to cool, stirring to eliminate any lumps.

Named after our chef, who is its creator, this recipe won a major award in Paris in 1982. For these apple-filled crêpes the chef recommends either a Golden Delicious or a Granny Smith, as they do not disintegrate while cooking. Both are slightly acid, and their hint of tartness goes perfectly with the taste of cider.

A spoonful of Calvados in your sabayon will enhance the flavor of the fruit. The added alcohol is negligible, so you can give the dessert to children without concern. Champagne could also be used instead of cider. Whichever you choose, the sabayon is served separately as a sauce.

These crêpes are so light that they are appropriate at any time, even at the end of a rather rich meal. They are particularly good for children, since they are energy-giving and rich in calcium, and are easily digestible, thanks to the fiber and acids provided by the apple. Serve them hot from the oven because, like soufflés, they shrink as they cool.

Enhance your guests' enjoyment with a bottle of good dry cider!

3. Separate the eggs, setting aside the whites. Add 2 yolks to the mixture in the pan. Whisk vigorously.

4. Whisk the egg whites into soft peaks. Using a wooden spatula, gently fold them into the mixture in the saucepan.

with Cider Sabayon

5. Drain the chopped apple; when completely cool, add to the filling mixture.

6. Fill the crêpes with a heaped spoonful of the apple mixture, fold, and bake 10 minutes in a hot oven. For the sabayon, vigorously whisk 3 eggs, the superfine sugar, cider and Calvados over low heat. Serve the crêpes hot with the frothy sabayon sauce.

1. Carefully peel, core and wash the fruit. Cut the large fruit into thin slices.

Ingredients:

Fruit in season:
1 apple, 1 pear,
   2 mandarin
   oranges, 2 kiwis,
   5 strawberries,
   1 handful
   raspberries,
   1 bunch grapes,
   1 small pineapple
4 egg yolks
1½ cup plus 3 tbsp/
   170 g sugar
¾ cup/170 ml dry
   white wine
⅓ cup/50 g confec-
   tioners' sugar
mint leaves, for
   decoration.

Serves 4
Preparation time: 25 minutes
Cooking time: 5 minutes
Difficulty: ✶

2. Arrange the fruit in an attractive pattern on an oven-proof dish. For the sabayon, whisk the egg yolks and sugar together vigorously in a saucepan.

Watching one's weight—what a bore! How hard it is to resist all those delicious little sweet desserts and mouthwatering treats. So, just for once, forget the diet and let yourself be led astray by this gorgeous concoction. It is so light, fresh and colorful, covered with its frothy sabayon sauce, that no one could possibly feel guilty about eating it!

Select your fruit assortment according to the season and your fancy. Whatever you choose will provide plenty of health-giving vitamins.

This fruit gratin should be served hot, immediately after removing it from under the grill. Just enjoy it, without worrying about your figure. It makes the perfect end to a festive meal and, if you are on a strict diet, it cannot help but cheer you up.

You will certainly feel like drinking something special with this delightful dessert, so go ahead and uncork a nicely-chilled Champagne Veuve Clicquot brut.

3. Place the saucepan over, but not in, simmering water and continue to whisk the egg yolks. Gradually add the white wine, still stirring.

4. Continue whisking the mixture over the heat until it is completely smooth and creamy. Do not allow it to stick to the bottom of the pan.

Gratin

5. When it begins to thicken, pour the sabayon over the fruit arrangement.

6. Sprinkle the platter with confectioners' sugar. Place under the grill for a few seconds, decorate with mint leaves, and serve immediately.

Chocolate

1. To make the mousse, begin by melting the chocolate over hot water. Add the butter, 3 tbsp/50 g of the sugar, and the egg yolks. Beat together very vigorously and allow to cool.

2. Whisk the egg whites to soft peaks with the remaining 2 tbsp/30 g sugar; then fold them into the cooled chocolate mixture.

Ingredients:
ladyfingers
For the mousse:
5¼ oz/150 g semi-
    sweet baking
    chocolate
10 tbsp/150 g butter
5 tbsp/80 g superfine
    sugar
5 eggs, separated
*For the crème
    anglaise:*
3½ tbsp/50 g
    superfine sugar
2 cups/500 ml milk
6 egg yolks

Serves 6
Preparation time: 20 minutes
Cooking time: 15 minutes
Chilling time: 4 to 5 hours
Difficulty: ✶

Some of the good things in life may be gone forever, but there are still plenty of traditional culinary delights that been preserved for us.

Here are a few tips for this marvelous dessert: Buy ready-made ladyfingers and moisten them with Grand Marnier or Cointreau. When making the mousse, melt the butter and chocolate completely before adding the sugar and egg yolks. Above all, remember that the yolks will cook unless you whisk them continuously and energetically. A pinch of salt in the egg whites will prevent them from becoming grainy.

To simplify removing the charlotte from the form, cut out a circle of aluminum foil slightly larger than the bottom of the form so that it extends about ⅜ in/1 cm up the sides. For an impressive finishing touch, decorate the charlotte with a chocolate design. Draw an outline on parchment paper, and use a pastry bag to create your design. Or think how delighted your children will be if you ask them to create a decoration for you.

This dream of a dessert is simple to make and suitable for any kind of gathering, informal or formal.

With your Chocolate Charlotte, serve Grand Marnier or a well-chilled Champagne Veuve Clicquot Etiquette Jaune.

3. Place a circle of aluminum foil in the bottom of a form and arrange the ladyfingers around its edge. (The ladyfingers can first be moistened with alcohol or a syrup.)

4. Turn the chocolate mousse into the form and chill in the refrigerator for 4 to 5 hours.

Charlotte

5. For the crème anglaise, heat the sugar in a until it caramelizes. When it is nicely colored, pour in the milk and bring to a boil.

6. Place the egg yolks in a bowl, pour the caramel milk onto them and whisk vigorously. Return the mixture to the saucepan and cook over low heat. Allow to cool. Serve the charlotte accompanied by chilled caramel crème anglaise.

Chocolate

1. For the génoise, break the eggs into a large bowl. Add the sugar and whisk vigorously until the mixture has doubled in volume. Sift the cocoa, flour and starch and combine, then gently fold into the eggs and sugar.

Ingredients:
For the génoise:
6 large eggs
1 cup/250 g superfine
    sugar
6½ tbsp/45 g bitter cocoa
¾ cup plus 1 tbsp/
    95 g flour
3 tbsp plus 2 tsp/30 g
    cornstarch
For the fondant:
1½ generous cups/375 g
    whipping cream
6½ oz/180 g semi-sweet
    baking chocolate
3½ tbsp/50 ml white rum
cocoa for decoration

Serves 6
Preparation time: 30 minutes
Cooking time: 20 minutes
Chilling time: 3 hours
Difficulty: ✶

Are you mad about sweet pastries and chocolate? Do time-consuming, complicated recipes discourage you? If they do, here, especially for you, is the ideal gâteau: delicious, but very simple to make. What's more, chocolate is rich in folic acid, vitamin B1, iron, and magnesium.

Take care to whip the cream to no more than three-quarters of a chantilly. Also, you must blend the chocolate and cream very rapidly, and add it immediately to the batter.

There is no need to pick at your food during the earlier courses to leave room for this dessert, since it is so light and dreamy. No one will be able to resist it, and it makes a beautiful finish to any kind of meal.

Chocolate does not go well with wines, but it is wonderful with Banyuls: Your guests will be delighted to make this discovery.

2. Thoroughly butter a cake pan, dust lightly with flour, and pour in the batter. Bake the génoise in a preheated 390° F/200 °C oven for about 15 to 20 minutes.

3. While the génoise is baking, prepare the fondant. Whisk the cream to ¾ of a chantilly, then place in the refrigerator.

4. Once the génoise has cooled, slice it horizontally, moisten each layer with a little white rum, place both halves in a cake ring, and set aside. Melt the baking chocolate at 104 °F/40 °C.

Fondant Gâteau

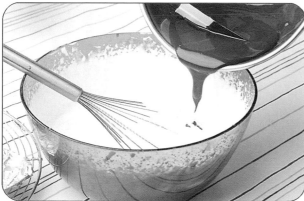

5. Let the chocolate cool slightly, then quickly fold it into the whipped cream. Whisk together vigorously.

6. Working very quickly, spread this mixture over the génoise and carefully smooth the surface. Refrigerate for 3 hours. Release the gâteau from the cake ring and sprinkle with cocoa.

Lemon

Ingredients:
10½ oz/300 g sablée
    pastry (see basic
    recipe)
zest of 3 lemons,
    grated
5 eggs
¾ cup/180 g sugar
1 cup/250 ml lemon
    juice
5¼ oz/150 g heavy
    cream

Serves 6
Preparation time: 35 minutes
Cooking time: 40 minutes
Difficulty: ✶ ✶

1. Make the sablée pastry, incorporating the lemon zest into the dough. Line a tart form with the pastry, and prick the bottom of the pastry shell with a fork.

2. To prevent the dough from rising while it bakes, place a sheet of aluminum foil on the pastry and cover with a layer of dried beans or ceramic baking beads. Bake in a hot oven for 15 to 20 minutes.

The brilliant yellow of the lemon recalls the sun, whose east-to-west course it has followed. Originating in India, the lemon was familiar to the Assyrians and Persians. The Greeks employed it both as a condiment and as a medicine. It was brought to western Europe by Crusaders returning from Palestine in the Middle Ages.

If you follow the chef's instructions closely you will have no problem with this delicious lemon tart. Rich in vitamin C, the dessert is very simple to make. It only requires a little care in mixing the ingredients. When properly baked, the filling will be soft and creamy on the bottom, and light and frothy on top.

Let the pastry rest in the refrigerator for three to four hours to make it easier to handle. Whip the cream well and fold it gently into the sugar-egg mixture. Bake the tart immediately after pouring the filling into the pastry shell. Using a wide, shallow tart or flan ring (about 12½ in/32 cm in diameter and 1½ in/3 cm high) will make it easier to release the tart.

With its fresh, rather sharp taste, your Lemon Tart will be just right at the end of a substantial meal. Depending on the circumstances, this dessert could be served with either a scented tea or a good Calvados.

3. Add the sugar to the eggs. Whisk together vigorously into a very well-blended paste.

4. Add the lemon juice, stirring continuously.

Tart

5. Whisk the light cream three-quarters of the way to a chantilly and add to the sugar and egg mixture.

6. Remove the foil and beans or beads from the pastry shell. Fill with the lemon cream mixture and bake in a very low oven for 20 to 25 minutes.

Brown Sugar

1. To make the soufflé, place the brown sugar in a bowl and break 3 eggs into it. Add the flour and stir together.

2. Pour the milk into a saucepan. Add the juniper berries and allow them to infuse while bringing the milk to a boil. While it is boiling, pour the milk onto the brown sugar mixture, stirring briskly all the time.

Ingredients:
6 ladyfingers
For the soufflé:
⅔ cup/120 g dark
   brown sugar
9 eggs
½ cup plus 2 tbsp/
   75 g flour
1½ cups/350 ml milk
12 juniper berries
3½ tbsp/50 ml juniper
   brandy
¼ cup/60 g sugar
*For the caramel
   sauce:*
6½ tbsp/100 g sugar
⅓ cup/80 ml water
2 cups/500 g crème
   fraîche

Serves 6
Preparation time: 25 minutes
Cooking time: 20 minutes
Difficulty: ✶ ✶

Brown sugar is made from the syrup produced in the process of refining either sugar beet or sugar cane. There are two types available, light and dark, and the latter has a stronger, more intense flavor.

Brown sugar gives this soufflé a lovely dark golden color and wonderful flavor that cannot be achieved with white sugar. Our chef has chosen juniper for its flowery fragrance, which will fill your kitchen even before you take the soufflé out of the oven. As an alternative, you might substitute cloves for the juniper berries—but do not add too many, for they have a very strong flavor.

If there are children among the guests, it would be a shame to deprive them of this marvelous dessert, a specialty of Picardy. So, on this occasion, you might omit brandy. This plump soufflé, rising proudly above the rim of its dish, must be eaten immediately. As everyone knows, soufflés cannot be kept waiting, otherwise they collapse miserably. But there is no danger here: You and your guests will lose no time in devouring this mouthwatering dish.

Serve the Brown Sugar Soufflé with a juniper brandy or a pale beer.

3. Return the mixture to the saucepan, and heat again while whisking continuously, until the preparation becomes thick and creamy. Remove from the heat and allow to cool.

4. For the sauce, prepare a caramel with the sugar and water. When it turns a lovely amber color, gently fold the crème fraîche into it, stirring with a wooden spatula. Allow to thicken for a few seconds over low heat. Remove from heat and set aside.

Soufflé

5. To complete the soufflé, separate the remaining 6 eggs and stir the yolks into the cooled brown sugar mixture. Add half the juniper brandy and blend thoroughly. Whisk the egg whites to soft peaks, then fold them gently into the soufflé mixture.

6. Butter a soufflé dish, sprinkle it with superfine sugar, and fill with half the soufflé mixture. Moisten the ladyfingers with the remaining juniper brandy, lay them on the soufflé, then add the rest of the mixture. Bake for about 20 minutes in a moderate oven and serve with the caramel sauce.

Pear

1. To prepare the filling, mix together the superfine sugar and powdered cream.

Ingredients:
1 génoise (see basic recipe)
16-18 ladyfingers
6 pears in syrup
2 cups/500 ml pear brandy
For the filling:
½ cup/125 g superfine sugar
½ cup/125 g powdered cream
1 cup/250 ml milk
8½ tbsp/130 g butter
To garnish:
6½ tbsp/100 g almond paste
⅔ cup/100 g confectioners' sugar

Serves 8
Preparation time: 30 minutes
Cooking time: 5 minutes
Chilling time: 3 hours
Difficulty: ✶ ✶ ✶

2. Bring the milk to a boil. Pour it into the sugar and powdered cream, whisking continuously. Stir vigorously until smooth and allow to cool.

The charlotte is a renowned classic, loved by gourmets of all generations. Here is just one of the numerous variations possible with this delectable dessert.

Be sure to whisk the butter into the cream vigorously, preferably with an electric mixer, to blend and aerate the mixture properly. Add the butter to the sugar and milk mixture while it is still slightly warm in order to give it just the right consistency. Also, take care to moisten the génoise with the alcohol syrup so that the charlotte is not too dry.

The charlotte should be very firm before you remove it from the cake ring. If your grill is weak, just sprinkle the surface with confectioners' sugar and serve. But here is a little trick that our chef is delighted to pass on to you: If you have a propane torch, direct the flame at the surface of the charlotte for a few seconds to brown it. You will be surprised—it really works!

Like all sweet pastries, this fruity charlotte requires a little care, but this light and exquisitely fragrant dessert will brighten your table all year round and enable you to end that special dinner on a high note.

Discover the pleasure of drinking fruit-based brandies with desserts, and serve a small glass of well-chilled pear brandy.

3. Drain and slice the pears; set aside the syrup. Slice the génoise into 3 layers.

4. Cut the butter into small pieces and gradually add it to the lukewarm sugar-milk mixture, whisking vigorously to blend.

Charlotte

5. Add the brandy to the pear syrup, and use it to moisten the génoise layers and ladyfingers. Place one layer in the bottom of a cake ring and line the sides of the ring with the ladyfingers. Spoon half of the filling onto the bottom layer of génoise and arrange half the sliced pears on it.

6. Repeat with the second layer. Top with the third layer of génoise. Refrigerate for 3 hours until firm. Remove the cake ring, then roll out the almond paste and cover the charlotte. Place under a grill for a few moments, dust with confectioners' sugar and serve.

Mirror of Pears

1. Bring the water, wine, and ¾ cup plus 1 tbsp/200 g of the sugar to a boil. Peel the pears and simmer them in the wine syrup over low heat. When cool, slice and carefully remove the cores, leaving an oval hole. Drain on a clean cloth; reserve the syrup.

2. Slice the génoise horizontally into 3 layers and trim to fit inside a cake ring.

Ingredients:
4 cups/1 liter water
2 cups/500 ml white wine
1¼ cups plus 2 tbsp/ 325 g superfine sugar
6 pears
1 chocolate génoise (see basic recipe)
3 egg yolks
1 cup/250 ml milk
8 leaves gelatin
1¼ cups/300 ml heavy cream
3½ tbsp/50 ml pear brandy

Serves 8
Preparation time: 45 minutes
Cooking time: 35 minutes
Chilling time: 6 hours
Difficulty: ✳ ✳ ✳

La Belle Hélène, immortalized in the Offenbach opera, inspired a number of chefs on the fashionable boulevards of Paris to dedicate some of their best creations to her. One of the most renowned of these dishes is Pears Belle-Hélène.

Rub the peeled pears with a lemon half to prevent them from discoloring. They will cook better if they are already sliced, but remember that they must remain firm; otherwise they will disintegrate because they are handled quite a lot in this recipe.

The plastic wrap must be stretched taut to produce a beautiful mirror-smooth surface. To unmold the gâteau, dip a pastry brush in hot water and run it several times around the outside of the form, which will then slide off easily.

This sophisticated dessert requires a bit of effort, but it is well worth it. You can simplify the preparation by buying a ready-made génoise and using canned pears.

Mirror of Pears Belle-Hélène can be frozen—but then you sacrifice its lovely shiny appearance. After removing it from the refrigerator, heat up a clear apricot or quince jelly to glaze the gâteau—it will look sensational!

Our wine expert loves to serve brandy with dessert and suggests introducing your guests to this pleasurable experience: Offer them a small glass of very fresh pear brandy.

3. Sort out enough well-formed pear slices to decorate the top and sides of the gâteau. Cut out small pieces of cake from the trimmings to fit inside the cored pears.

4. In a bowl, mix the egg yolks and 5 tbsp/75 g sugar. Bring the milk to a boil and pour it over the egg yolks and sugar to make a crème anglaise. Add the rest of the pear trimmings to this custard and mix thoroughly. Dissolve the gelatin in a little water and whisk it into the crème anglaise while it is still hot.

Belle-Hélène

5. Whisk the cream and the remaining sugar into a chantilly (see basic recipe). Fold it into the cooled crème anglaise to produce a bavarois, and blend in the pear brandy. Moisten the génoise layers with the wine syrup in which the pears were cooked.

6. Line a cake ring with plastic wrap. Arrange the pear slices on the bottom and sides of the ring. Pour in ⅓ of the bavarois and cover with a layer of génoise. Repeat twice more, ending with a layer of bavarois. Refrigerate for 5 to 6 hours and turn out onto a platter.

Old-Fashioned

1. Roll out the puff pastry. Cut a circle 8-10 in/20-25 cm in diameter. Prick the pastry with a fork and place it on a baking sheet.

Ingredients:
5¼ oz/150 g puff pastry
  (see basic recipe)
10½ oz/300 g choux
  pastry (see basic
  recipe)
1 egg yolk
*For the crème Saint-
  Honoré:*
2 cups/500 ml milk
1 vanilla bean
4 egg yolks
½ cup/60 g flour
Italian meringue
  (see basic recipe)
For the caramel:
6½ tbsp/100 g superfine
  sugar

Serves 6
Preparation time: 90 minutes
Cooking time: 35 minutes
Chilling time: 3 hours
Difficulty: ✶ ✶ ✶

2. With a pastry bag, draw a spiral of choux pastry on the circle of puff pastry. In addition, form about 20 small balls of choux pastry.

Parisian in origin, this gâteau is said by some to have been named in honor of the patron saint of bakers and *pâtissiers*, or pastry chefs. Others believe that the pâtissier who invented it had his shop on rue Saint-Honoré in Paris. These two theories are not mutually exclusive; but whatever its real history, this dessert is undoubtedly worthy of its great reputation. In fact, it often serves as a showcase for pastry chefs to demonstrate their abilities.

You can use a short pastry or another pastry for the base as long as it does not contain too much sugar, for a choux pastry must be baked for a relatively long time, and a high sugar content would cause the base to burn.

Allow the steam to escape from the oven by leaving the door slightly ajar. This will prevent the choux pastry, which rises very rapidly, from collapsing just as quickly.

Our chef recommends storing the egg whites for the meringue in the refrigerator for several days, but no longer than 8 days. Well-chilled and not freshly-laid eggs will be much easier to whisk than fresh eggs.

To accompany this queen of desserts, you could serve a sweet—but not too sweet—white wine, such as a Tokay d'Alsace or a Côteaux du Layon. But it is also delicious with tea or fruit juice.

3. Brush the surface of the choux pastry balls with beaten egg yolk, then lightly flatten them with a fork. Bake the pastry circle and little balls (on a separate baking sheet) in a hot oven until golden.

4. Prepare a pastry cream (see basic recipe) with the milk, vanilla bean, 4 egg yolks and flour. After it cools, fold it into the chilled Italian meringue. Blend together gently to form the crème Saint-Honoré.

Saint-Honoré

5. Make a caramel with the superfine sugar, and use it to fix the choux pastry balls onto the circle of puff pastry. Coat each ball with a spoonful of caramel.

6. With a pastry bag, fill the interior of the pastry ring with the crème Saint-Honoré. Refrigerate for 2 to 3 hours and serve very cold.

Iced Praline Dauphin

1. In a saucepan combine the water, port and sugar and bring to a boil to form a port syrup.

Ingredients:

4 tsp/20 ml water
⅔ cup/150 g port
½ cup plus 2 tbsp/
150 g sugar
3½ oz/100 g praline
2 cups/500 ml heavy
cream
3½ oz/100 g praline
paste
8 egg yolks
12 small meringues
To garnish:
chocolate sauce (see
basic recipe)

Serves 6
Preparation time: 45 minutes
Cooking time: 5 minutes
Chilling time: 5 hours
Difficulty: ✶ ✶

2. Crush the praline; whisk the cream into a chantilly (see basic recipe). In a bowl, combine 2 tbsp crème chantilly with the praline paste; whisk thoroughly to a smooth consistency.

As its name proclaims, this is a sumptuous and regal dish, and deserves to be among your very favorite desserts. Sabayon is an impossibly light and frothy wine cream that originated in Italy, where it is known as *zabaione*, or *zabaglione*.

To make the sabayon, whisk the egg yolks very gently over a double boiler while pouring in the port and sugar syrup. You must be very careful when cooking a sabayon. When the eggs have thickened well, they are done. Continue beating off the heat until they have cooled completely. You can use an electric mixer, if you prefer, and if it needs to go quickly you can cool the sabayon more rapidly by placing the pan in a large bowl filled with ice or iced water.

This parfait could be served with a caramel crème anglaise instead of a chocolate sauce. In any case, this impressive dessert is worthy of your most important guests.

Our wine expert suggests a vintage port, which you could serve in the English fashion from a crystal decanter.

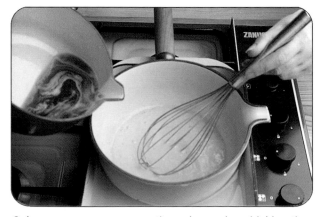

3. In a saucepan, prepare the sabayon by whisking the egg yolks in the top of a double boiler over warm, not boiling, water. Pour the port syrup onto the egg yolks and continue to beat briskly. Remove from heat and continue to whisk until cooled.

4. Add the crushed praline to the créme chantilly, combine with the praline paste mixture, and stir together gently.

with Port Sabayon

5. Add the cooled port sabayon to the praline-chantilly mixture and blend together gently.

6. Fill a mold with alternate layers of the praline mixture and small meringues, and freeze for 5 to 6 hours. Turn the iced praline out of the mold, decorate as desired, and serve with a chocolate sauce.

Profiteroles with

1. On a slightly dampened baking sheet, form approximately 36 choux profiteroles using a pastry bag with a plain nozzle.

2. Beat the egg yolk with a little water, and slightly flatten each profiterole with a fork dipped in the beaten egg yolk.

3. For the chocolate sauce, melt the chocolate in a bain-marie, then stir in the milk and heavy cream. Heat the sauce briefly, then set aside.

Ingredients:
- 10½ oz/300 g choux pastry (see basic recipe)
- 1 egg yolk
- 2 cups/500 ml vanilla ice cream

For the chocolate sauce:
- 8¾ oz/250 g semi-sweet baking chocolate
- ½ cup/125 g milk
- ½ cup/125 g heavy cream

For the chantilly cream:
- ¾ cup/200 g heavy cream
- 3½ tbsp/50 g superfine sugar
- confectioners' sugar to decorate

Serves 6
Preparation time: 30 minutes
Cooking time: 25 minutes
Difficulty: ✳ ✳

The word *profiterole* originally referred to any kind of little treat, not just edible ones; since the 16th century, however, it has been used only in the culinary sense.

This particular dessert, the Rolls-Royce among pastries, is over 100 years old.

The success of the recipe depends on the choux pastry, of course. Refer to our basic recipe to ensure that yours turns out well. It is essential to stir the butter and water together very briskly. Add the salt and sugar, and allow the dough to dry out a little on the stovetop. It is ready when it comes away cleanly from the sides of the pan. Then you can beat in the eggs, one by one, away from the heat.

Choux pastry does not stick, so there is no need to grease the baking sheet. Since the amount of crème chantilly used is so small, you might prefer to use ready-made chantilly as well as ready-made ice cream.

This is a much-loved classic and you, too, are assured great popularity if you treat your friends to it.

It is difficult to find any suitable wine to go with this gorgeous dessert with its contrast of hot and cold, so our wine expert suggests serving a fine Arabica coffee.

4. Bake the profiteroles in a medium-hot oven until they have risen and turned golden brown. Meanwhile whisk together the heavy cream and the sugar to make a crème chantilly (see basic recipe).

Chocolate Sauce

5. Allow the profiteroles to cool, then carefully slice off a "lid" from each.

6. Fill the profiteroles with vanilla ice cream, cover, and top the lids with chantilly. Sprinkle with confectioners' sugar and serve with hot chocolate sauce.

Chocolate Sorbet

1. To make the sorbet, pour the water into a saucepan, add the superfine sugar and bring to a boil.

Ingredients:

For the sorbet:
4 cups/1 liter water
1 cup plus 3 tbsp/300 g
    superfine sugar
4¼ oz/150 g
    unsweetened cocoa
3¾ oz/80 g invert sugar
3½ oz/100 g heavy
    cream
For the crème anglaise:
bouquet of mint
2 cups/500 ml milk
5 egg yolks
¾ cup plus 1 tbsp/200 g
    sugar
Tuile baskets (see *pâte à
    tuiles* basic recipe)

Serves 6
Preparation time: 30 minutes
Cooking time: 20 minutes
Chilling time: 30 minutes
Difficulty: ✴ ✴

2. Cook over low heat for about 3 minutes, then add the cocoa. Stir in the trémoline and allow to cool.

If you love unexpected combinations of flavors to surprise your gourmet friends, you will be delighted with this sophisticated sorbet. As confectioners know, the combination of fresh mint and dark chocolate is particularly pleasing.

There are several kinds of mint, but peppermint is the most strongly scented and is frequently used in cooking and the preparation of various alcoholic drinks. One could also try lemon mint or bergamot for their fruity taste.

According to Greek legend, Pluto, husband of Proserpine, fell in love with Minthe. After finding Minthe with her husband, Proserpine took revenge on her rival by turning her into a plant.

To make sure the sorbet will be perfect, choose a bitter chocolate, because it has a stronger flavor than sweet chocolate. Above all, do not overcook the chocolate mixture or it will become too thick: Just let it melt, without boiling. Also, let the mint thoroughly infuse in the milk.

This delicious and refreshing dessert, so freshly scented, will provide a beautiful end to any type of meal. It is not easy to find the right drink to go with it, but our wine expert is sure that a Champagne Henriot will be able to hold its own.

3. When this mixture has cooled, stir in the cream, then pour into an ice cream maker and churn until very well-blended. Place the sorbet in the freezer.

4. Strip the mint leaves from the stalks. Carefully wash and finely chop the leaves.

with Mint Sauce

5. For the crème anglaise (see also the basic recipe), bring the milk to a boil, add the chopped mint and allow to infuse.

6. Combine the sugar and egg yolks, beat vigorously, then add the hot milk while continuing to whisk. Allow the custard to cool. Place balls of chocolate sorbet in tuile baskets and serve with the minted crème anglaise.

Fritters

1. Sift the flour into a mixing bowl, add the yeast and stir to combine.

Ingredients:
4 generous cups/
   500 g flour
1 package yeast
a pinch of salt
4 tsp/20 g superfine
   sugar
3½ tbsp/50 ml
   Burgundy marc
1 tbsp cooking oil
zest of 1 lemon
4 eggs
6½ tbsp/100 g butter,
   softened
oil for frying
confectioners' sugar
   for decoration

Serves 10
Preparation time: 15 minutes
Cooking time: 30 minutes
Chilling time: 3 hours
Difficulty: ✶

In France these fritters are traditionally eaten on special feast days, particularly on Shrove Tuesday. As far back as the Middle Ages vendors from Arles to Dijon sold them in the open air, but eventually they became known as a specialty of Lyon.
Pay attention to the dough: Measure the ingredients very accurately, as the correct proportions are important. Knead the dough until it no longer sticks to the pastry board. Then let it rest in the refrigerator for two to three hours to become firm before rolling it out. Only then will you be able to roll it thinly enough to produce excellent fritters.
In reality, fritters are quick and easy to make, so why wait for Shrove Tuesday? Children, who know what is good, are sure to keep pestering you to make them. With such a delicious treat, every day is a holiday!
Our wine expert recommends a Champagne brut Veuve Clicquot. With its fine bubbles, this great champagne will make the festive occasion even more enjoyable.

2. Add the salt and sugar, and mix again.

3. Pour the Burgundy marc and cooking oil into the dry ingredients; stir. Add the lemon zest.

4. Add the eggs, one at a time, beating until very well-blended after each addition.

Lyonnaise

5. Knead the dough thoroughly with your hands, then work in the well-softened butter. Continue kneading until perfectly smooth. Place the dough in the refrigerator to rest for 2 to 3 hours.

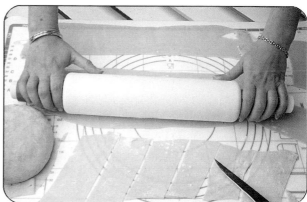

6. Divide the dough into 6 pieces, and roll them out very thinly. Cut into strips. Heat the oil in a deep pan, then drop the strips of dough into it. Drain, dust with confectioners' sugar and serve.

Smooth

Ingredients:
3 scant cups/450 g
  confectioners'
  sugar
2 cups/250 g ground
  blanched almonds
1½ cups/250 g egg
  whites
3½ tbsp/50 g
  superfine sugar
3 tbsp marmalade

1. Carefully sift the confectioners' sugar, then add it to the ground almonds and stir together.

Serves 6
Preparation time: 20 minutes
Cooking time: 20 minutes
Difficulty: ✫ ✫ ✫

2. Whisk the egg whites with the superfine sugar until soft peaks form.

Legend has it that in the 18th century macaroons were made in various monasteries and were said to look like monks' navels! The macaroons made in Nancy are supposed to be the best of all, and at one time they were made by Carmelite nuns who, even if they had withdrawn from the world, certainly had not abandoned all the pleasures of life. During the French Revolution, two sisters in particular became famous for the macaroons they produced and came to be known as the *soeurs macarons*.

Use finely ground almonds and well-sifted confectioners' sugar. The sugar and almond mixture must be completely dry, otherwise the macaroons will tend to crack in the oven. The mixture should also be slightly warm before being added to the whisked egg whites, so put it in front of the half-open oven door for a while to dry out.

If you follow all the instructions carefully, the macaroons will be perfect! Do not be too disappointed if they are slightly cracked and not quite as smooth as they should be—they will nonetheless be beautifully soft inside.

These morsels are delicious eaten at any time of day and are just the thing if you are feeling a bit tired around tea time or coffee time.

3. Fold the almond and sugar mixture into the whisked egg whites and blend very carefully with a spatula.

4. Using a pastry bag with a plain nozzle, form small macaroons on a sheet of parchment paper. Bake until golden brown in a moderate oven, leaving the door slightly ajar during baking.

Macaroons

5. Remove the macaroons from the oven. To lift them from the parchment paper, pour a little water between the baking sheet and the paper, or place the paper on a well-dampened surface for about 10 minutes

6. Spread a little marmalade on the bottom of each macaroon, then stick 2 together, and enjoy.

Lacy

1. Cut the grapefruit in half, squeeze the juice from them, and set aside.

Ingredients:
3 grapefruit
1¼ cup/150 g flour
2½ cups/250 g flaked
 almonds
3⅓ cups/500 g
 confectioners'
 sugar
1 cup/250 g butter

Serves 6
Preparation time: 20 minutes
Cooking time: 10 minutes
Difficulty: ✶ ✶

2. Sift the flour, then stir in the flaked almonds.

What could be finer than these marvelous *tuiles*! It would be convenient if they could just to drop onto your plate, but our talented *pâtissier* has been kind enough to let us into the secret of his recipe. In his version, this thin, crisp and delicate cookie, curved like a Roman tile (which is precisely what *tuiles* means in French) has been refined with the fresh, slightly sharp taste of grapefruit. Alternatively, you can use orange, which also produces a delicious result.

Our chef says that the dough will be easier to handle if you make it a day or two in advance and then allow it to rest in the refrigerator.

The dough will then be a very soft, almost liquid paste. Place it in the freezer for a few minutes to make it firm. When you take the tuiles out of the oven, wait 30 to 40 seconds before molding them around a rolling pin to give them the desired shape.

Whether as tidbits at an enjoyable tea party, or as a special snack for the children, or with sorbet or chocolate, these Grapefruit Tuiles are bound to be a great success.

3. Add the sifted confectioners' sugar to the flour and almonds and mix well.

4. Pour the grapefruit juice over the dry ingredients and stir to combine.

Grapefruit Tuiles

5. Melt the butter, add it to the mixture, and stir thoroughly. Butter a baking sheet and dust with flour. Form each tuile by dropping a spoonful of the mixture onto the baking sheet and flattening it with a fork dipped in cold water.

6. Bake the tuiles in a moderate oven and after 20-30 seconds drape them over a rolling pin to cool into a curved shape. Serve with ice cream or an iced dessert.

Chocolate

1. Prepare the chocolate puff pastry, referring to the basic recipe and replacing 10% of the flour with unsweetened cocoa powder. Roll it out into thin sheets and bake.

Ingredients:
14 oz/400 g chocolate
  puff pastry
⅔ cup/80 g bitter cocoa
2½ tbsp/50 g pistachio
  paste
2 cups/500 ml crème
  anglaise (see basic
  recipe)
5 leaves gelatin
1 cup/250 ml crème
  chantilly, unsweetened
  (see basic recipe)
⅓ cup/50 g confectioners'
  sugar
chocolate sauce (see
  basic recipe)

Serves 4
Preparation time: 1 hour 30 minutes
Cooking time: 10 minutes
Chilling time: 2 hour
Difficulty: ✭ ✭ ✭

The *millefeuille*, also known as Napoleon, is a classic sweet pastry with a long history; here it has the added novelty of a pistachio cream. Who could resist the dark beauty of these sheets of puff pastry with their succulent pale green filling? But the recipe requires time and special care in order to achieve a perfect result.

Start with a dark, almost red, cocoa powder. If you like, follow our chef's example and replace the sugar in the crème anglaise with 2½ tbsp/60 g honey, which produces a deliciously sweet and creamy mixture.

Prick the puff pastry with a fork before baking so that it rises evenly.

Use a wooden spatula to help you assemble your pastries, because they are very fragile and will crumble unless they are handled carefully. And now you can sit back and wait for the praise that is bound to come your way.

Our wine expert suggests a Maury to go with the Chocolate Pistachio Millefeuilles. This wine's intense cocoa and dark caramel flavors will be subtly enhanced by the taste of the chocolate pastry.

2. Add the pistachio paste to the crème anglaise. Whisk briskly until the paste has thoroughly dissolved.

3. Dissolve the gelatin in a little cold water, drain, and add to the pistachio crème anglaise. Stir vigorously, then allow to cool.

4. When the pistachio crème anglaise has cooled, but before it solidifies, fold it into the crème chantilly. Place it in the refrigerator to set.

Pistachio Millefeuille

5. Cut the sheets of chocolate puff pastry into rectangles 2x4 in/5x10 cm, and set aside for 2 hours.

6. Spread ⅔ of the pastry rectangles with pistachio cream and stack them on top of each other to make each millefeuille. Dust with confectioners' sugar and serve with cold chocolate sauce.

Hot Caramelized

1. On a baking sheet, use a pastry bag to form choux pastry rings.

Ingredients:
7 oz/200 g choux pastry
  (see basic recipe)
1 egg yolk
6 Golden Delicous
  apples
5 tbsp/75 g butter
⅓ cup/80 g superfine
  sugar
¼ cup/40 g confectioners'
  sugar
¾ cup/200 ml vanilla ice
  cream
¾ cup/200 ml heavy
  cream
pinch grated nutmeg
1 tsp ground cinnamon
mint leaves to garnish

Serves 4
Preparation time: 25 minutes
Cooking time: 15 minutes
Difficulty: ✳ ✳

2. Mix the egg yolk with a little water and brush the surface of the pastry rings with it. Bake in a moderate oven for about 20 minutes.

This appealing dessert, with its regal appearance, will give a royal finish to any kind of meal, whether simple or grand.

The cinnamon, with a spicy smell reminiscent of its eastern origins, brings out the flavor of the apples. It also has a very long history, and is even mentioned in the Bible. Over the centuries it has been used to flavor wines, meat and fruit. In eastern Europe it is still widely used, and the Viennese cinnamon cakes are truly delicious. On the other side of the Atlantic, it seems that an apple dessert without an additional dash of cinnamon is almost inconceivable.

Our chef recommends using Golden Delicious apples if possible, because they remain very firm when cooked, and that you pipe the choux pastry onto a buttered baking sheet, forming crowns 3¼ in/8 cm in diameter.

Even after a hearty meal, who could resist the appeal of this mouthwatering concoction of pastry, fruit, and ice cream?

Our wine expert suggests a Calvados: The combination of apple liqueur with hot apples is a pleasure not to be missed.

3. Peel and core the apples. Slice half of them, and dice the rest.

4. In a frying pan, sauté the diced apples in 3 tbsp/45 g of the butter. When they are half-done, sprinkle them with the superfine sugar and allow to caramelize slightly. Sprinkle with a pinch of nutmeg.

Apple Crowns

5. Arrange the apple slices on a buttered baking sheet. Dust with a little confectioners' sugar and place under the grill until the sugar caramelizes.

6. Slice the choux pastry crowns in half horizontally. Fill sandwich-fashion with the diced apples, and cover with overlapping slices of caramelized apple. Crown with ice cream and garnish with mint leaves. Serve on a bed of cream flavored with cinnamon.

Poire

1. Slice off a piece of the bulb of each pear to provide a flat base.

Ingredients:
4 large ripe pears
  with stems
1 lemon
4 cups/1 liter water
¾ cup plus 1 tbsp/
  200 g superfine
  sugar
¾ cup/200 ml vanilla
  ice cream
6½ tbsp/100 ml heavy
  cream
1 tbsp confectioners'
  sugar
chocolate sauce
  (see basic recipe)
8 mint leaves

Serves 4
Preparation time: 20 minutes
Cooking time: 10 minutes
Difficulty: ✶

2. Cut off a similar piece from the opposite side of each pear.

This classic dessert, with its musical and frivolous connotations, has always been a great favorite. Make your guests happy by serving them with this gastronomic operetta. You will find that this intriguing Belle-Hélène, which looks so splendid, is actually very easy to prepare.

Our chef advises you to choose pears that are large, fragrant and well-ripened, but make sure that they are firm.

Do not neglect to rub lemon over the pears; otherwise they will discolor. Moreover, the acidity of the lemon will add a very pleasant, sharp note to the flavors of pear and vanilla ice cream. Leave the pears in the syrup to cool, but remember that they will continue cooking as long as the syrup is still hot; check them frequently to ensure that the pears do not become too soft.

To add a finishing touch, decorate the chocolate sauce with a pattern drawn in crème fraîche. The contrast of light and dark will give the dessert an even more showy appearance, striking the right chord at even the grandest reception.

Our wine expert recommends a Banyuls Grand Cru (Domaine du Mas-Blanc), to set off this great classic dessert.

3. Using a knife and a spoon, scoop out the flesh from the bulb of the pear, removing the core and seeds. Immediately rub the flesh of the fruit with half a lemon to avoid discoloration.

4. Combine the water and sugar; bring to a boil and cook 15 minutes to produce a syrup. Squeeze the juice of the lemon into the syrup and poach the pears in it for 10 minutes. Allow the pears to cool in the syrup.

Belle-Hélène

5. When the pears are completely cooled, carefully drain them and fill with ice cream.

6. Whisk the cream into a chantilly with the confectioners' sugar, and pipe it on top of the pears. Serve with a hot chocolate sauce, and decorate with mint leaves.

Apple

1. Separate the eggs.

Ingredients:
6 egg yolks
6½ tbsp/100 g sugar
1¼ cups/300 ml
  sweet cider
6½ tbsp/100 ml heavy
  cream
6 apples
3½ tbsp/50 g butter
3½ tbsp/50 ml
  Calvados
sugar to sprinkle on
  apples

Serves 4
Preparation time: 20 minutes
Cooking time: 20 minutes
Difficulty: ✶

2. Add the sugar to the egg yolks and whisk vigorously
for several minutes until they become pale.

This dessert from Normandy is simple and direct, both in its preparation and its taste.
There are many varieties of apple to choose from, but our chef recommends Golden
Delicious because they stay firm during cooking. But you may wish to substitute a
regional apple with good cooking qualities.

Take care when pouring the boiling cider on the egg yolks. You must do this very swiftly
and smoothly while whisking vigorously, otherwise the yolks will cook and the mixture
will be ruined. Also, this operation must be carried out away from the heat.

If you prefer, the cider crème anglaise can be prepared a day in advance and stored in the
refrigerator until needed.

This dessert induces a happy, relaxed mood and is ideal at the end of a family meal. The
warm amber color of a good Calvados, such as Calvados du Père Magloire, would go
well with it, as would, of course, a flagon of cider

3. Bring the cider to a boil in one saucepan and heat
the cream in another. Pour the hot cider onto the egg
yolks and sugar mixture while whisking vigorously.

4. Pour the hot cream onto the mixture. Whisk, return
to the pan, and cook to produce a crème anglaise
(see basic recipe). Remove from heat.

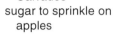

Gratin

5. Peel and slice the apples; melt the butter in a frying pan and brown the apples in it. Sprinkle some sugar over them and allow to caramelize.

6. Flambé the apples in the Calvados. Arrange the apples on a serving dish, cover with the cider sauce, and place under the grill for 3 minutes. Serve very hot.

1. Add the condensed milk to the caramel. Stir together and set aside.

Ingredients:
7 oz/200 g
    sweetened
    condensed milk
6½ tbsp/100 ml dark
    liquid caramel,
    cooled
½ cup/125 g sugar
⅔ cup/150 ml heavy
    cream
6 egg yolks
1⅔ cups/400 ml milk
2 vanilla beans

Serves 8
Preparation time: 30 minutes
Cooking time: 15 minutes
Freezing time: 45 minutes
Difficulty: ✶

2. Bring the sugar and cream to a boil in a saucepan. Allow to simmer until the mixture caramelizes.

This iced caramel treat recalls the enchantment of childhood. Indeed, the medieval Latin word *cannamella* literally means "honey-water reed."

Heated above 300°F /150° C, sugar syrup changes color; the darker it is the less intense its sweetness. For this recipe, allow the syrup to become a dark caramel to flavor the crème anglaise. After the caramel is finished and has cooled considerably, add a little water to make it more liquid.

This recipe takes rather a long time to prepare but, at any time of year, your patience will be repaid by the happy faces around the table—those of the grown-ups as well as the children. Moreover, this desert is good choice for children because it is energy-giving and rich in calcium.

Our wine expert warns that caramel has a tendency to "fight" with wine. However, you can create harmony by serving a Champagne rosé Veuve Clicquot or—be daring—a big glass of ice water!

3. Whisk the egg yolks in a bowl. Place the vanilla beans in the milk, bring it to a boil and immediately pour the milk onto the egg yolks while continuing to beat vigorously.

4. Return the mixture to the saucepan and simmer gently, still whisking continuously, to produce a thick crème anglaise (see basic recipe).

Caramel Chiffon

5. Add the caramel and cream mixture from Step 2 to the crème anglaise. Stir together vigorously.

6. Add the dark caramel and condensed milk mixture to the mixture and blend well. Allow to cool, then pour into an ice cream maker. Churn until creamy, then serve.

Plum

1. Roll out the pastry and line a tart pan with it. Prick the pastry all over with a fork.

Ingredients:
- 10½ oz/300 g sablée pastry (see basic recipe)
- 2.2 lbs/1 kg plums (*quetsches*)
- 6 eggs
- 10 tbsp/100 g ground almonds
- ¾ cup/200 ml heavy cream
- 3½ tbsp/50 g butter
- 6½ tbsp/100 g sugar
- 1 tbsp confectioners' sugar
- 1 tsp vanilla extract
- 1 tbsp quetsch brandy
- flour

Serves 6
Preparation time: 20 minutes
Cooking time: 40 minutes
Difficulty: ✮

2. Halve the plums and remove the stones. Set aside the fruit.

The *quetsch* is a variety of plum widely grown in France, especially in Alsace. Its sweet, strong flavor and juiciness make it ideal for tarts and cakes. No matter what variety you use, choose plums that are ripe but firm. Use smooth and fruity quetsch brandy to add flavor to the custard.

Make the sides of the tart high, because the custard is very liquid and there is the chance that it will overflow during cooking. Leave the oven door slightly open while baking to prevent the pastry from becoming soggy.

The tart is best served warm, but do let it rest for a quarter of an hour before bringing it to the table.

Any stone fruit can be used in this recipe. Whole fruit, with the stone left in, will stay more juicy and keep its flavor better. Try it and see!

This delicious tart can be served on all kinds of occasions and is guaranteed to win an enthusiastic following.

To correspond to the regional character of the tart, our wine expert suggests a Tokay d'Alsace. This great dry wine will gently counteract the sweetness of the plums, while enhancing their flavor.

3. Break the eggs into a bowl. Whisk slightly, and then add the ground almonds.

4. Pour the cream into the egg and almond mixture and whisk together vigorously.

Tart

5. Melt the butter and, together with the sugar, stir it in.

6. Arrange the halved plums in the pastry shell. Stir the vanilla and brandy into the cream mixture, spoon the filling into the tart, and bake about 40 minutes in a moderate oven. Before serving, sprinkle with confectioners' sugar.

Iced Raspberry

1. Stone the cherries and dice them finely. Whisk the cream into a chantilly and set aside.

Ingredients:
2 ladles morello
   cherries with syrup
6½ tbsp/100 g vanilla
   ice cream
3½ tbsp/50 ml kirsch
2 cups/500 ml
   raspberry sorbet
¾ cup/200 ml
   raspberry coulis
   (see basic recipe)
6½ tbsp/100 ml heavy
   cream
For decoration:
mint leaves
fresh raspberries

Serves 6
Preparation time: 15 minutes
Freezing time: 1 hour
Difficulty: ✶

2. Allow the vanilla ice cream to soften a little, then incorporate the diced cherries.

Morello cherries are those small sour cherries which are not always easy to find the year round; fortunately, they are still delicious when canned. Buying the ice cream ready made will also save a lot of time and make this a particularly easy recipe to make.

The chef advises you to strain the raspberry coulis to make it thinner and filter out the plentiful little seeds that crunch between the teeth. Raspberries are a fruit that can even be eaten by diabetics, because of the particular qualities of their sugar.

You can vary this dessert as the fancy takes you: Make it with melon, cherry or pear sorbet, or with mint or chocolate ice cream. If you choose pear sorbet, use pear brandy instead of kirsch. Anything is possible—just give your imagination free rein to dream up a surprise or two.

Like all iced desserts, this one keeps well in the freezer and can be brought out as a splendid treat to please children. It is deliciously fragrant and is an ideal way of ending a rather substantial meal on a fresh and light note.

Our wine expert suggests serving a Champagne Veuve Clicquot.

3. Stir the kirsch gently into the ice cream, then return the ice cream to the freezer.

4. Allow the raspberry sorbet to soften, then spoon some of it into a cake ring or mold. Bring the sorbet up the sides, leaving a hollow in the middle.

and Cherry Gâteau

5. Fill the hollow with the ice cream and cherries, and return to freezer until the ice cream and sorbet become firm again.

6. Fill the cake ring with a layer of raspberry sorbet, smoothing the top carefully. Return to the freezer to harden. Just before serving, turn the gâteau out onto a plate. Decorate with raspberries and mint leaves, and serve with raspberry coulis and a little crème chantilly.

Hot Fruit Tart

1. Roll out the puff pastry and cut out 4 circles the size of a small crêpe. Prick each one with a fork and bake in a hot oven.

2. Turn the pastry cream into a blender. Add the chopped almonds and sugar and blend.

Ingredients:
7 oz/200 g puff
   pastry (see basic
   recipe)
⅔ cup/150 g pastry
   cream (see basic
   recipe)
scant ¾ cup/125 g
   chopped almonds
3½ tbsp/50 g
   superfine sugar
1 green apple
1 banana
8 strawberries
1 pint raspberries
plums, peaches,
   cherries
confectioners' sugar
raspberry coulis (see
   basic recipe)

Serves 4
Preparation time: 25 minutes
Cooking time: 5 minutes
Difficulty: ✷

What makes this tart especially delicious is the medley of fruits with their contrasting tastes and textures, as well as the pleasurable sensation of slight sourness provided by the raspberries.

Almonds are a very nutritious and energy-giving foodstuff, especially recommended for pregnant and nursing mothers.

After rolling out the pastry and cutting out tart bases, it is important to let the pastry rest for 10 minutes in the freezer, or 20 minutes in the refrigerator.

For perfect pastry, our chef recommends baking the rounds in two stages: Start by putting them in a very hot oven for ten minutes, without the fruit, which would make it soggy. Then arrange the firmer kinds of fruit on the rounds, and complete the baking. Soft fruits such as strawberries and raspberries should not be added to the tarts until after they are baked. When served, these fruits will be warm but not cooked. You can also use apricots, wild strawberries, pears—whatever is in season can be combined to make a gloriously sweet and juicy confection.

Follow all this advice carefully, and you will have no difficulty in producing a feast for the palate and for the eyes. This colorful dessert, all bright yellow and red, is absolutely irresistible for young and old alike! Our wine expert recommends a Champagne Henriot to accompany it.

3. Clean, peel and slice the various fruits as necessary, removing stones and seeds.

4. Spread a tablespoonful of the almond cream onto each pastry circle.

with Raspberry Coulis

5. Arrange the fruit in a pattern on top of the cream.

6. Dust the tarts with confectioners' sugar and place in a hot oven for a few seconds. Serve encircled with raspberry coulis.

Melon

1. Slice the génoise horizontally into 2 layers and set them aside. Add the sugar to the heavy cream and whisk together into a crème chantilly (see basic recipe).

Ingredients:
1 génoise (see basic recipe)
3½ tbsp/50 g sugar
1 cup/250 ml heavy cream
1 cup/250 ml pastry cream (see basic recipe)
1 melon
juice of 1 orange
1 cup/250 ml sugar syrup
1 wine glass Muscadet wine
3 tbsp red currant jelly

Serves 6
Preparation time: 30 minutes
Chilling time: 3 hours
Difficulty: ✶✶

2. Add ¾ of the crème chantilly to the pastry cream and gently blend to make the filling for the gâteau. Peel the melon and slice it thinly, reserving some melon flesh for decoration.

Originally native to Asia, the melon was already known in China 1,000 years B.C., and in Ancient Egypt as well.

Charles VIII of France discovered the melon growing on a papal estate in Italy. He introduced it in France, where it was enthusiastically cultivated by the popes at Avignon. During the reign of the Sun King, royal botanists worked to improve the varieties at Versailles. Another fan of this lovely juicy fruit was Alexandre Dumas, author of *The Three Musketeers*, who claimed he would rather have been paid for his work, not in jingling, cumbersome money, but in beautiful big melons!

Choose the melon for this recipe carefully: A strong sweet smell can disguise over-ripeness; rather it should weight heavily in your hand and have a thick, supple and unblemished skin.

Melon Gâteau, which will keep for two days in a cool place, will be particularly welcome in the heat of high summer.

In the opinion of our wine expert, the extreme sweetness of this dessert calls for a rash move: Uncork an extra-dry champagne, such as a Veuve Clicquot. You could also opt for a Muscat-de-Baumes-de-Venise.

3. Add the orange juice and sugar syrup to the Muscadet and mix together. Use a pastry brush to moisten the génoise with this syrup.

4. Cover one layer of the génoise with filling.

Gâteau

5. Arrange the melon slices on the cream, and top with the second layer of génoise.

6. Melt the red currant jelly and generously cover the top of the gâteau with it. Set it in the refrigerator to become firm. Coat the sides of the cake with the remaining filling. Decorate with melon balls and the reserved crème chantilly.

Pumpkin and

1. Peel the pumpkin and cut it into large cubes.

Ingredients:
7 oz/200 g pumpkin
½cup plus 1 tbsp/
   100 g ground
   almonds
6½ tbsp/100 g sugar
zest of 1 orange
12½ oz/350 g puff
   pastry (see basic
   recipe)
confectioners' sugar
   for decoration

Serves 6
Preparation time: 25 minutes
Cooking time: 45 minutes
Difficulty: ✳

2. Cook the pumpkin with a little water in a covered saucepan over low heat.

The pumpkin is a vegetable native to the New World, and is a member of the squash family. In America it appears on dining tables primarily in the form of a custard in pumpkin pie, an essential part of the traditional Thanksgiving Day feast.

Pumpkins are ready for picking from October to December, but they can also last right through the winter. In Provence, this tart is traditionally eaten at Christmas.

Select a pumpkin with a deep golden orange color. Steam it for 20 minutes so that it becomes less watery. Remember to brown the ground almonds under the grill to bring out the richness of their flavor. Instead of orange zest, the tart could be flavored with lemon zest or vanilla.

Once the tart is baked, sprinkle it with confectioners' sugar and then let it brown under the grill for a few moments to give it a wonderfully appetizing glaze.

The tart can be served warm or cold, but do not refrigerate it because this will make the pastry lose its crispness and become soggy.

Brighten up the cold, gray days of winter by serving this golden dessert.

To go with the Pumpkin and Almond Tart, open a bottle of good, very dry champagne. Our wine expert recommends a *champagne non dosé*, to which no sugar has been added during the fermentation process.

3. When it is tender, purée the pumpkin in an electric blender. Toast the ground almonds and add to the pumpkin purée.

4. Add the sugar and orange zest to the pumpkin mixture and blend very thoroughly. Leave to cool.

Almond Tart

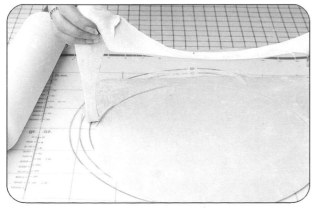

5. Roll out the puff pastry into a circle with a diameter of about 12 in/30 cm. Lightly pinch it around the edges.

6. Spread the pumpkin purée mixture over the pastry. Cover with the rest of the pastry cut into a lattice pattern. Bake the tart in a moderate oven for about 25 minutes. Sprinkle with confectioners' sugar, and serve warm.

Williams Pear

1. In a saucepan, heat the sugar and water until a syrup is formed.

Ingredients:
¾ cup plus 1 tbsp/ 200 g superfine sugar
⅔ cup/150 ml water
2 lemons
1 cup/250 ml white wine
2½ tbsp/40 ml pear brandy

Serves 4
Preparation time: 10 minutes
Cooking time: 15 minutes
Chilling time: 25 minutes
Difficulty: ✶

From its wild origins in Asia Minor, the pear tree came very early under cultivation. Pears were highly regarded in particular by the Romans, who enjoyed them as fruit and also developed a fermented drink from them. There are a very large number of pear varieties, but today it is the Williams pear that is used for making pear brandy.

This sorbet has an intense aroma of pears, and since its delicate fragrance comes from the pear brandy, make sure to choose a good one. For the syrup, you can use a dry white wine, a Cassis or a Châteauneuf.

The sorbet must be served very cold, of course, so leave it in the freezer until the last moment. Decorate the dessert with a few mint leaves or a small candied pear.

This recipe, so quick and simple to make, and so delicious to eat, is very refreshing on the hottest days of summer or after a substantial meal.

A glass of pear brandy, well-chilled, is a must here. The clink of ice cubes against the glass adds to the enjoyment.

2. After the syrup has cooled, squeeze the lemons and stir the juice into it.

3. Pour in the white wine and stir to combine.

4. Add the pear brandy and blend again.

Sorbet

5. Transfer the mixture to the ice cream maker. Add the ice cubes and coarse salt, if necessary, and turn.

6. Arrange sorbet balls in a serving dish and sprinkle with a little pear brandy before serving.

Nut

1. For the fond de succès, combine the confectioners' sugar, ground hazelnuts and ground almonds. Add the flour and superfine sugar and mix well. Whisk the egg whites into stiff peaks, then gradually blend the dry mixture into them.

2. On a lightly buttered baking sheet, use a pastry bag to pipe one large fond de succès disk and several smaller ones. Bake for 20 minutes.

Ingredients:
⅔ cup/100 g confectioners' sugar
4½ tbsp/50 g each: ground hazelnuts and almonds
10 tbsp/75 g flour
6½ tbsp/100 g superfine sugar
4 egg whites
1 cup/250 ml pastry cream(see basic recipe)
½ cup plus 1 tbsp/100 g ground almonds
10 tbsp/150 g butter
1 cup/250 ml crème anglaise (see basic recipe)
1¾ oz/50 g pistachio paste
cocoa powder
confectioners' sugar

Serves 6
Preparation time: 35 minutes
Cooking time: 15 minutes
Chilling time: 1 hour
Difficulty: ✸ ✸

In French culinary terminology, a *fond* can be a stock, or a base for a gâteau or dessert. The *fond de succès* that forms the base of this Nut Gâteau derives its name from its tradition as a reputation-maker for aspiring pastry chefs. It is one of the great classics of the marvelous French gastronomic repertoire.

Our chef says that to produce perfect fond de succès bases it is helpful to trace the approximate outline of the cake on the baking sheet, using a cake ring or pastry-cutters. This circle is brushed with melted butter, then dusted with flour. The circles are then filled, or piped, with the mixture, using a pastry bag. To ensure neat disks, start at the center of each circle and hold the bag quite high.

The meringue must be very stiff and as dry as possible. Otherwise the almonds and hazelnuts, which contain a certain amount of water, could render the mixture too liquid and cause it to collapse. Do not whisk the pastry cream for too long or it will start to go "grainy," as if the butter had begun to turn.

Hazelnuts are full of calories but they are also rich in nutrients such as folic acid, zinc, potassium and magnesium.

This mouthwatering gâteau will make all food-lovers swoon with pleasure. It certainly is a *gâteau du succès*.

Our wine expert feels only a bottle of good champagne will do the Nut Gâteau justice.

3. Prepare a chiffon cream by gently heating the pastry cream, then vigorously whisking in the ground almonds. Allow the cream to cool.

4. Once the cream has cooled to room temperature, gradually blend in the well-softened butter with an electric mixer.

Gâteau

5. Place the large fond de succès base in a cake ring and fill with the chiffon cream. Refrigerate until firm.

6. Sprinkle half of the small fond de succès disks with cocoa powder and the other half with confectioners' sugar. Arrange them on top of the gâteau. Mix the pistachio paste with the crème anglaise, and serve with the gâteau.

Kiwi, Banana and

1. Cut the bananas into thin slices and sauté them quickly in butter. As soon as they start to brown, sprinkle with 2½ tbsp/40 g of the sugar and continue stirring over the heat until caramelized.

Ingredients:
14 oz/400 g bananas
⅔ cup plus 5 tbsp/ 190 g sugar
6½ tbsp/100 ml aged rum
3½ tbsp/50 ml corn syrup
6½ tbsp/100 ml crème fraîche
½ cup/125 g butter
2 egg whites
3-4 kiwis
1 génoise (see basic recipe)
syrup for moistening the gènoise

Serves 6
Preparation time: 40 minutes
Cooking time: 20 minutes
Difficulty: ✷ ✷

2. Pour the rum onto the bananas and flambé. Allow to cool slightly; then blend them in a food processor to produce a banana paste.

This pretty, fruity dessert, with its lovely caramel flavor, is quite irresistible and is sure to become a favorite.

The chef advises to use very little sugar when browning the banana slices. The caramel added later will provide all the sweetness needed. Prepare it at the same time as the bananas, so that the two mixtures are both warm when you combine them in order to avoid lumps.

Be careful not to add too much caramel, because it is important not to mask the taste of the bananas, which is absolutely essential. With the leftover caramel mixture you could have some fun: Make soft caramel candies by leaving it to set between two sheets of parchment paper or waxed paper.

The addition of butter to the banana caramel ensures that the mixture stays slightly soft when it has cooled, otherwise it will be too hard when set.

Decorate the Saint-Agne with slices of banana or kiwi fruit. Meringue also adds a sophisticated finishing touch.

Ideal for a children's party or a birthday party, this dessert is energy-giving and rich in potassium and vitamin C.

To go with the Saint-Ange, children can drink a glass of fruit juice, while the adults might prefer to enjoy a Champagne Veuve Clicquot Carte Jaune.

3. Pour the rest of the sugar into a saucepan, add the corn syrup, and stir over low heat to produce a caramel. When the caramel turns amber, stir in the crème fraîche and allow it to cook.

4. Gradually add the caramel-crème fraîche mixture to the banana paste, blend with an electric mixer, and allow to cool.

Caramel Saint-Ange

5. Once it has cooled completely, gradually add the butter, cut into small pieces. Blend well. Whisk the egg whites until they form stiff peaks.

6. Slice the génoise horizontally into 2 layers, moisten them with a little syrup, and spread the cream filling on the bottom layer. Cover with the second layer and top with the beaten egg whites. Place under the grill for a few seconds, then garnish with half-slices of kiwi fruit all around the sides.

Banana and

1. Combine the water, slit-open vanilla bean, and 1 cup/250 g of the sugar in a saucepan and heat to make a syrup.

Ingredients:
2 cups/500 ml water
1 vanilla bean
1⅗ cups/400 g sugar
4 bananas
4 clementine oranges
4 eggs
1 glass champagne
flaked almonds

Serves 4
Preparation time: 20 minutes
Cooking time: 15 minutes
Difficulty: ✶ ✶

2. Peel the bananas and the clementines. Slice the bananas and segment the clementines. Cook the banana slices in the syrup; after 5 minutes add the clementines and leave in the syrup for a further 3 minutes. Drain the fruit and set it aside.

Fruit gratins provide a fresh, colorful feast, and winter is just the season when we often feel the lack of such splendor; luckily, our chef has had the excellent idea of creating a winter-fruit gratin.

For the vanilla bean to flavor the syrup as strongly as possible, make an incision in it with the point of a knife before adding it to the syrup. Drain the fruit after poaching it in the syrup; otherwise the sabayon could become too liquid. Cooking the sabayon in the top of a double boiler is less risky, but experienced cooks do so directly over the heat. Watch the sabayon carefully and stir constantly to prevent it from burning.

You might enjoy creating rosettes or other patterns out of the fruit on top of the sabayon, or simply conceal all the fruit underneath it to give your guests a lovely surprise.

There are other kinds of fruit you could use, such as pineapple or grapefruit—it is up to you to find the most tempting combination.

Our wine waiter recommends serving a Champagne Veuve Clicquot Carte d'Or, which will combine magnificently with the frothy sabayon.

3. Separate the eggs. Place the yolks in a double boiler, add the rest of the sugar, and whisk over the heat to obtain a creamy sabayon.

4. Pour in the glass of champagne while continuing to whisk vigorously.

Clementine Gratin

5. Spread the flaked almonds on a baking sheet and brown under the grill, stirring them from time to time.

6. Arrange the fruit attractively on an oven-proof serving dish. Cover it with the sabayon, sprinkle with toasted almonds, and brown in the oven for a few minutes. Serve hot.

Iced Honey Nougat

Ingredients:
1 orange
8 egg yolks
4½ tbsp/100 g honey
1 cup/250 g sugar
1 cup/100 g flaked
  almonds
2 cups/500 ml heavy
  cream
2¾ oz/80 g diced
  candied fruit
½ cup/125 ml caramel
  sauce

Serves 6
Preparation time: 40 minutes
Cooking time: 10 minutes
Chilling time: overnight
Difficulty: ✳✳

1. Remove the zest from the orange and julienne it finely. Blanch in a generous amount of water. Whip the egg yolks thoroughly with an electric mixer.

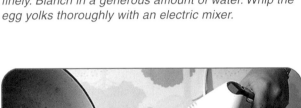

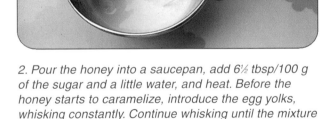

Montélimar is the capital of nougat, and its confectioners have always been regarded as the greatest specialists in making it. However, also in Provence, nougat is one of the thirteen desserts traditionally served at Epiphany as a symbol of fecundity.

Our chef recommends a liquid pine honey which smells wonderfully of the Jura mountains. The toasted almonds should be nicely browned and crunchy.

Professional cooks use a candy thermometer when making a caramel. Note that soft caramel is done when the temperature reaches 250° F/121° C. In the absence of a thermometer, a good approximation is to boil the sugar, honey and water mixture over moderate heat for five minutes.

Blend the egg yolks until very pale before adding them to the warm caramel. Allow the mixture to cool before folding it into the whipped cream.

The orange zest should cook for about 10 minutes in the sweetened orange juice. For the caramel topping, prepare a caramel and when it starts to turn light brown, add a little water to it to stop the cooking. Then reheat it again over very low heat. Allow it cool, then add the poached zest.

Serve the dessert frozen, preferably chilled overnight. Whether solo or accompanied by crisp petits fours and a Veuve Clicquot Grande Dame Champagne, Iced Honey Nougat is an elegant finish to dinner or a delightfully sophisticated note to afternoon tea.

2. Pour the honey into a saucepan, add 6½ tbsp/100 g of the sugar and a little water, and heat. Before the honey starts to caramelize, introduce the egg yolks, whisking constantly. Continue whisking until the mixture is cooled.

3. Spread the flaked almonds on a baking sheet and toast under the grill. Allow to cool. Whisk the heavy cream into a crème chantilly (see basic recipe), then gently fold in the honey and egg yolk mixture with a wooden spatula.

4. Add the cooled flaked almonds and candied fruit, and stir together gently.

with Orange Sauce

5. Fill a charlotte or soufflé mold with this nougat mixture. Place in the freezer to chill overnight.

6. Squeeze the orange, and add the remaining sugar and a little water to the juice. Simmer the julienned zest in this syrup, then mix it with the softened caramel sauce. Top the nougat with the caramel.

1. Line a hemispherical mold with a ¾ in/2 cm-thick layer of chocolate ice cream. Place in the freezer.

Ingredients:
2 cups/500 ml chocolate ice cream
For the chocolate mousse:
5 tbsp/75 g sugar
4 egg yolks
½ cup/125 g milk
2½ oz/75 g Caraque (or if necessary, other unsweetened baking chocolate)
7½ tbsp/110 g heavy cream
chocolate shavings for decoration

Serves 6
Preparation time: 20 minutes
Cooking time: 10 minutes
Freezing time: 3-4 hours
Difficulty: ✴ ✴

2. Add the sugar to the egg yolks and whisk together vigorously. Bring the milk to a boil. Pour it over the egg yolks and sugar, stirring continuously. Transfer the mixture to a saucepan and cook as a crème anglaise (see basic recipe).

Our chef has named his decadent creation Le Caraque after the dark, strongly-flavored Valrhona chocolate much prized by confectioners. It has a superior taste and texture that will leave a strong impression on anyone experiencing it for the first time.

Crème anglaise must be cooked over low heat and stirred constantly with a whisk. Our chef advises you to keep whisking the crème anglaise and chocolate mixture until it has cooled completely. This will ensure a light and delicious mousse when the chocolate custard is combined with the crème chantilly. To avoid lumps, always add the thinner component—in this case the chocolate custard—to the thicker. Introduce the crème anglaise slowly to prevent the mixture from becoming too liquid.

If you do not have a hemispherical form, you can use any other shape you like. To turn out the dessert more easily, dip the mold in hot water for a few moments when you take it out of the freezer.

Chocolate! How the word rolls happily in the mouth! Le Caraque will give unforgettable pleasure to all chocolate-lovers.

It is well known that wine and chocolate do not mix well; however, you might try a drop of Banyuls with this dessert.

3. Break up the chocolate and put it in a saucepan. Pour the hot crème anglaise over the chocolate, and stir vigorously until the chocolate has completely melted and the mixture has cooled.

4. Whisk the heavy cream into a chantilly (see basic recipe) and gently fold the cooled chocolate custard into it.

Caraque

5. Remove the mold lined with chocolate ice cream from the freezer and fill the hollow with the chocolate mousse. Freeze for 3 or 4 hours.

6. Just before serving, turn the dessert out of the mold and, if you wish, coat with a thick chocolate syrup. Decorate with chocolate shavings.

Iced

1. Heat the sugar with a few drops of water until melted. Bring to a boil and cook for 3 or 4 minutes to the "soft ball" stage. Pour the boiling sugar syrup onto the egg yolks, whisking vigorously until the mixture has completely cooled.

2. Pour a little of this mixture onto the chestnut paste, add the rum, and stir until the paste is well softened. Combine this with the rest of the whisked egg yolks and sugar, and stir together until thoroughly blended.

Ingredients:
6½ tbsp/100 g sugar
4 egg yolks
3½ oz/100 g chestnut
   paste
3½ tbsp/50 ml aged
   rum
1 cup/250 ml heavy
   cream
2 cups/500 ml pear
   sorbet
pieces of glazed
   chestnuts
6½ tbsp/100 ml thick
   chocolate syrup
20 ladyfingers
3½ tbsp/50 ml pear
   brandy
6½ tbsp/100 ml sugar
   syrup

Serves 6
Preparation time: 20 minutes
Cooking time: 10 minutes
Freezing time: 4 hours
Difficulty: ✴ ✴

The original charlotte, which appeared in France in the late 18th century, was based on an English dessert possibly created in honor of Charlotte, wife of King George III.

Our chef's charlotte is sweet and fresh, and suitable for any time of year. Cooks keen on confectionery probably possess a candy thermometer and know that sugar boils at 233 °F/112 °C. In the absence of a thermometer, just let the sugar boil for a few minutes and then remove from the heat.

When you pour the boiling syrup onto the egg yolks, it is essential that you whisk the mixture continually with an electric mixer until it is completely cooled. To speed up the process, place the bowl containing the egg yolks in a basin of iced water.

Iced Charlotte is particularly suitable for brightening up the dull days of winter. Our chef also suggests a variation of this dessert, using champagne sorbet: A marvelous way of celebrating Christmas, for example!

If glazed chestnuts are not readily available, buy or make a rum-laced, vanilla-flavored chestnut paste.

Try a Champagne Veuve Clicquot rosé with this delicious dessert.

3. Whisk the cream into a stiff crème chantilly (see basic recipe) and gently fold into the chestnut mixture.

4. Place a cake ring in the freezer for several minutes, then line the bottom and sides with pear sorbet. Fill with the chestnut mixture, to which the sugared chestnuts have been added. Freeze for 2 hours, then top with the rest of the pear sorbet and return to freezer.

Charlotte

5. Cover the top of the frozen charlotte with chocolate syrup and return to the freezer to solidify.

6. Release the charlotte from the cake ring. Slightly moisten the ladyfingers with a mixture of the pear brandy and sugar syrup, and apply them to the sides of the charlotte.

Piedmontais

Ingredients:
5¼ oz/150 g
  hazelnuts
  (in their shells)
5 tbsp/75 g sugar
4 egg yolks
5 tsp/25 ml Cognac
6½ tbsp /100 g heavy
  cream
½ cup/125 g milk
2 cups/500 ml
  pistachio ice cream

1. Shell the nuts and grill them. Toast them in the oven and crush with a rolling pin. Add the sugar to the egg yolks and whisk vigorously. Beat the cream into a crème chantilly (see basic recipe), blend in the Cognac, and leave in a cool place.

Serves 6
Preparation time: 30 minutes
Cooking time: 10 minutes
Freezing time: 4 hours
Difficulty: ✳ ✳

Hazelnuts, like truffles, are typical products of the Italian Piedmont, in honor of which our chef has named his deliciously nutty dessert.

Stop cooking the crème anglaise just before it comes to a boil, as soon as bubbles start to appear on its surface. Pour it into a bowl and cool it by beating it with an electric mixer. If the eggs in the mixture start to curdle, simply whisk to eliminate the lumps. Do not worry about what sticks to the bottom of the pan.

Add the alcohol to the whipped cream, never to the crème anglaise, which would then collapse and become soft.

For the mousse, use a cake ring that is smaller in height and diameter than the one you line with ice cream. There is a risk that the mixture will leak out of the ring while you are filling it, so work quickly and place the filled ring immediately into the freezer.

Grill the hazelnuts before crushing them. If you like, they can be caramelized, or dusted with confectioners' sugar before roasting. You can have fun decorating the Piedmontais with chocolate shavings to set off the pale green of the pistachio. Your dessert will be the focal point of your dinner.

The tiny, delicate bubbles of a fine champagne served with this dessert will fill your guests with joy.

2. Bring the milk to a boil, pour into the egg yolks and continue beating. Return to the saucepan and cook as a crème anglaise (see basic recipe). Remove from the heat and whisk vigorously until the custard is completely cooled, then fold into the crème chantilly.

3. Arrange some of the grilled crushed hazelnuts in a small cake ring and then fill with the cream filling.

4. Sprinkle the rest of the nuts over the cream and place in the freezer for at least 2 hours.

5. Line a larger cake ring with pistachio ice cream. Turn out the frozen hazelnut cream onto the middle of the ice cream.

6. Top with a layer of pistachio ice cream and harden in freezer for at least another 2 hours. Just before serving, dip the ring quickly in hot water, turn out onto a platter, and serve decorated with chocolate shavings and shelled hazelnuts.

Vaucluse

1. To make the candied peaches, bring the peach juice and sugar to a boil. Dice the peach halves, add the diced fruit to the syrup, and boil a few more minutes. Allow to cool and refrigerate.

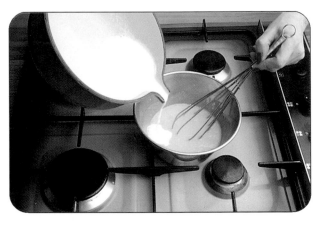

2. For the mousse, add the sugar to the egg yolks and whisk vigorously. In another pan, bring the milk to a boil and pour it onto the egg yolks, stirring constantly. Return to the saucepan and cook as a crème anglaise (see basic recipe). Remove from heat and cool.

3. Whisk the heavy cream into a stiff chantilly (see basic recipe), then add the maraschino liqueur. Fold the cooled crème anglaise into the crème chantilly, stirring gently until well-combined. Fold in some of the chilled candied peach.

Ingredients:
For the candied peaches:
½ cup /125 g peach juice (canned)
1 cup/250 g sugar
5 peach halves
For the iced mousse:
8 egg yolks
½ cup plus 2 tbsp/150 g sugar
1 cup/250 ml milk
¾ cup/200 ml heavy cream
2½ tbsp/40 ml maraschino liqueur
fruit glaze (optional)
2 cups/500 ml peach sorbet

Serves 6
Preparation time: 25 minutes
Cooking time: 30 minutes
Freezing time: several hours
Difficulty: ✳ ✳

Our chef has named this lovely fresh peach delicacy after the beautiful Vaucluse region, known for its abundant fruit.

The filling is made like a crème anglaise, rich in eggs and sugar. The egg yolks and sugar do not have to be beaten for very long. By contrast, after pouring the boiling milk onto the beaten eggs, you must whisk vigorously while this mixture is cooking and continue whisking until it is completely cooled. Using an electric mixer will help reduce the temperature quickly.

Whisk the heavy cream until it is firm, but stop as soon as it thickens. Do not let it turn into butter!

To combine these two elements to make the mousse, add the crème anglaise, which is the thinner of the two creams, to the crème chantilly. Be careful to pour it in gradually. If you work too quickly, the mousse will become too liquid. If you like, bake a disk of *pâte sablée* or *fond de succès* to cover the mousse and candied peach pieces. Then, when you turn out the sorbet, it will be sitting on a sweet pastry base.

The fruit glaze is not obligatory but it will please perfectionists! You could opt for pears or nectarines, either fresh or in syrup, as delicious variations for this glaze.

Our wine expert suggests you surprise your guests with a great French wine which deserves to be better known: Muscat de Rivesaltes.

4. Line a round mold with the peach sorbet and place in freezer to harden, then fill the form to the top with the mousse mixture. Return to freezer to harden slightly.

Peach Sorbet

5. Spread the rest of the candied peach cubes on the surface of the mousse, then return to the freezer for several more hours.

6. Just before serving, dip the mold quickly in hot water. Turn out the sorbet and coat with a thick, well-chilled fruit glaze.

Iced Whisky

1. For the ganache, melt the chocolate in a saucepan over very low heat.

Ingredients:
*For the whisky
  ganache:*
10½ oz/300 g semi-
  sweet baking
  chocolate
6½ tbsp/100 g milk
  chocolate
5 tbsp/75 ml heavy
  cream
2½ tbsp/40 ml corn
  syrup
⅔ cup/150 ml whisky
2 cups/500 ml vanilla
  ice cream
1 cup/110 g bitter
  cocoa powder

Serves 6
Preparation time: 30 minutes
Cooking time: 10 minutes
Freezing time: 30 minutes
Difficulty: ✯ ✯

This mouthwatering dessert will appeal to chocolate-lovers of all ages.

Our chef uses corn syrup rather than sugar to keep the ganache soft and prevent it from crystallizing. You will be able to squeeze it through the pastry bag with ease.

Another tip: Do not add the whisky to the ganache mixture until the chocolate has completely melted. You can speed the process up by stirring it. If you use another type of alcohol, choose a fruit brandy, rather than a liqueur.

It is helpful to thoroughly chill the cocoa in which the ice cream balls are rolled; otherwise your dessert may melt before you have finished preparing it! Your guests will enjoy discovering the truffle inside its casing of vanilla ice cream.

Every one adores champagne—so champagne all round! Our wine expert recommends a Champagne Veuve Clicquot Carte d'Or.

2. In a separate pan, combine the cream and corn syrup and bring to a boil.

3. Stir the hot sweetened cream into the melted chocolate and allow to cool slightly. Add the whisky and whisk thoroughly. Stir the ganache from time to time while it thickens.

4. Using a pastry bag with a plain nozzle, form little balls of the ganache on a sheet of parchment paper. Place in freezer for 30 minutes.

Truffles

5. Remove the ganache from the freezer and rub between your hands to form balls. Half-fill a small ice cream scoop with vanilla ice cream, place a ganache ball in the middle of it, then finish filling the scoop with ice cream.

6. Roll the ice cream balls in chilled cocoa powder and place in the freezer until ready to serve.

Apple Mousse with

Ingredients:
2.2 lbs/1 kg yellow apples
1¼ cups/300 g superfine sugar
6 egg whites
7 oz/200 g raspberries for the coulis (see basic recipe)

Serves 4
Preparation time: 20 minutes
Cooking time: 45 minutes
Difficulty: ✷ ✷

1. In a saucepan, melt 5 tbsp/75 g of the sugar and boil until it caramelizes. Pour a little of the caramel into the bottom of 4 ramekins or other ovenproof forms.

2. Peel, core and slice the apples. Place on a baking sheet and bake dry in the oven. When they are finished and quite dry, purée them in a food processor. Leave them in the bowl of the processor.

The apple is charged with symbolism and history: The forbidden fruit of knowledge in the Garden of Eden, Aphrodite's golden apple of discord which led to the fall of Troy, and the apples of Isaac Newton and William Tell are just a few examples. In French, one can *tomber dans les pommes*, meaning to faint from emotion, and in Quebec, lovers *chanter la pomme*, or "sing the apple" when they murmur sweet nothings.

If you are making this recipe in winter, the chef advises using a Reinette or Pippin apple; during the rest of the year, Golden Delicious is the best choice.

The caramel should be pale, so to halt the cooking, dip the bottom of the saucepan in iced water. Fold the whisked egg whites into the apples using a wide circular movement to prevent them from collapsing.

To check whether the mousses are ready, stick a knife blade into one of the portions. If it comes out completely dry, your mousse is finished.

The coulis can be made with any soft red fruit, using 7 oz/200 g of fruit sweetened with some sugar.

Whether served hot or cold, this is an excellent dessert for novice cooks who want to make an impression.

A little glass of Calvados Père Magloire would go magnificently with this mousse—just try it!

3. In a saucepan, melt ½ cup plus 2 tbsp/150 g sugar and heat it to the "soft ball" stage (just before it takes on a caramel color). Add this syrup to the apple purée and blend thoroughly.

4. Whisk the egg whites into soft peaks, adding the rest of the sugar. When the apple purée is cold, gently fold in the egg whites.

Raspberry Coulis

5. Fill the ramekins with the mixture, place in a bain-marie, and bake in a hot oven for 20 minutes.

6. Prepare a raspberry coulis according to the basic recipe, strain it, and pour onto the serving dish. Turn out the mousse, arrange on the coulis, and garnish.

Red Fruit Compote

1. Wash the currants, strawberries, raspberries and wild strawberries.

Ingredients:
- 7 oz/200 g strawberries
- 7 oz/200 g raspberries
- 7 oz/200 g wild strawberries
- 2 kiwi fruits
- 7 oz/200 g red currants
- 1 glass Champagne Veuve Clicquot
- 1 cup plus 2 tbsp/ 400 g red currant jelly
- 4 scoops vanilla ice cream
- mint leaves

Serves 4
Preparation time: 20 minutes
Difficulty: ✶

2. Peel the kiwis and cut into wedges.

There is such a wide variety of fruits—luscious and juicy, crisp and tangy, melting in the mouth, soft, firm, bursting with sweetness, pleasantly sharp, all full of subtle fragrance and taste. And there is no end to the range of delicious, light desserts to be made with them. The colors of the fruits used in this recipe, from light red to bright scarlet, strike a particularly cheerful note.

The fruit also provides a vitamin cocktail, especially vitamin C, making it a good dessert for children. It can be made in record time: In fact, no cooking is required. Choose the fruits according to taste and availability.

One small tip: Wash the strawberries with their stems intact, as they otherwise tend to fill with water and lose their delicious flavor.

If you are serving Red Fruit Compote to children, thin the currant jelly with lemon juice instead of champagne. For an excellent variation on this recipe, try mint sorbet instead of vanilla ice cream.

To drink with it, give the children a pure fruit juice, while the grown-ups can enjoy Champagne Veuve Clicquot rosé. The color of this great wine will nicely complement your summery dessert.

3. Add the champagne to the currant jelly and whisk it in thoroughly.

4. Cover the bottom of a serving dish with this sauce.

with Vanilla Ice Cream

5. Arrange the fruits in an attractive pattern on the sauce.

6. Add the scoops of vanilla ice cream, decorate with mint leaves, and serve very cold.

Pineau Ice Cream

1. Peel the melon, cut it in half, and remove the seeds. Cut the flesh into large cubes. Place them in a pan with half the sugar and a glass of water. Cover and cook over very low heat.

Ingredients:
1 generous lb/500 g firm yellow water-melon flesh
2 cups/470 g sugar
1 glass water
2 cups/500 g heavy cream
8 egg yolks
3½ tbsp/50 ml Cognac
6½ tbsp/100 ml Pineau
watermelon rind for basket

Serves 6
Preparation time: 30 minutes
Cooking time: 40 minutes
Freezing time: 12 hours
Difficulty: ✳ ✳ ✳

2. Skim the surface of the liquid from time to time. When the melon becomes soft, remove from heat and allow to cool in the syrup, then drain.

Many years ago, a wine grower needed a receptacle for some leftover wine. He poured it into a cask still containing a little distilled *eau-de-vie*. Imagine his surprise when he discovered the contents had clarified, producing a divine liquid to which he immediately gave his own name: Pineau. It has since become very typical of his native Charentes.

Our chef has chosen a small yellow-fleshed watermelon because its flesh is firm and cooks well. If you use another type of melon, remember that flesh that may be too soft and watery, and will disintegrate during cooking.

Cook the melon cubes over a very low heat. To keep the pieces whole, the syrup must not rise above a simmer. As always when pouring boiling liquid onto egg yolks, continue whisking the mixture vigorously during and after the operation to prevent them from becoming lumpy. The same is true for the cream.

Pineau Ice Cream with Candied Melon looks marvelous served in a "basket" cut out of the thick skin of the melon. This bright and cheerful dessert has a holiday air about it, and is perfect for the hot days of summer.

It demands to be savored slowly, while drinking—what? A nice glass of chilled Pineau des Charentes, of course!

3. Slightly beat the egg yolks in a bowl, then add the rest of the sugar, the Cognac and the Pineau. Whisk together very vigorously. Bring the cream to a boil.

4. Pour the boiling cream onto the egg yolk mixture while whisking vigorously.

with Candied Melon

5. Pour the cream mixture through a fine sieve into a saucepan and cook as a crème anglaise (see basic recipe). Continue to stir without pause so that it does not coagulate. Allow to cool.

6. Pour the cold cream mixture into an ice cream maker and churn until very firm. Serve accompanied by the pieces of candied watermelon.

Apple Marignan

1. Peel, core, and quarter the apples.

Ingredients:
10 yellow apples
¾ cup plus 1 tbsp/
  200 g sugar
1 glass water
7 oz/200 g sablée
  pastry (see basic
  recipe)
6 leaves gelatin
1 lemon
1 cup/250 ml heavy
  cream
6½ tbsp/100 ml
  apricot coulis
  (see basic recipe
  for coulis)
1 cup/250 ml caramel
  sauce

Serves 8
Preparation time: 20 minutes
Cooking time: 20 minutes
Chilling time: 4 hours
Difficulty: ✷ ✷

The name of this dessert derives from the Battle of Marignano in 1515, when Francs I reconquered Milan.

Some people might compare the launching into the preparation of a fancy French cream cake is something like engaging in a battle: Face the panic, muster your forces, then strike—but rest assured, this is a battle you will win.

Our chef recommends Golden Delicious apples because they cook well and produce a delicious compote. The gelatin will enable the apple Marignan to keep its shape when turned out of its form without altering the taste of the apple. Thus, the potential culinary disaster of a sadly collapsed gâteau is avoided.

Once you have achieved this astonishing success, you will want to prepare the Marignan again and again, perhaps with bananas instead of apples. Either way, you are bound to score a great victory and win your friends' admiration!

This magnificent dessert deserves a really good champagne; our wine expert recommends opening a Champagne brut Veuve Clicquot for this special occasion.

2. Cook the apples together with the sugar and a glass of water until the apples are soft. Stir frequently while cooking.

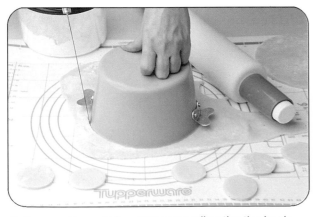

3. Prepare the sablée pastry according the the basic recipe, roll it out, and cut out a disk to fit inside a cake form. Bake in a moderate oven and set aside.

4. Dissolve 1 leaf of gelatin in the apricot coulis, and whisk until completely dissolved. Pour into the form and refrigerate.

with Caramel Sauce

5. Blend the apples into a purée, adding the rest of the gelatin and the juice of the lemon. Set aside to cool. Whisk the heavy cream into a firm chantilly (see basic recipe).

6. Gently fold the crème chantilly into the apple puree. Turn into the form and refrigerate about 4 hours. Cover with the pastry disk, turn out onto a cake platter, and cover with apricot coulis. Serve very cold with a caramel sauce.

Caramelized

1. Carefully peel and core the apples, then quarter them lengthwise.

Ingredients:
10 tbsp/150 g butter
½ cup plus 2 tbsp/
   150 g sugar
8 Golden Delicious
   apples
10½ oz/300 g puff
   pastry (see basic
   recipe)
2 tbsp flour for pastry
   board

Serves 6
Preparation time: 15 minutes
Cooking time: 35 minutes
Difficulty: *

2. In a fairly deep oven-proof dish, melt the butter and sugar together.

This recipe is bound to seem familiar to you, and with good reason: It is none other than the famous Tarte Tatin, given a new name by our chef.

The Misses Tatin were two sisters who owned a restaurant in Sologne at the beginning of the 20th century, and who unwittingly created the dessert when they dropped an unbaked tart upside down. They decided to bake it anyway, and the result was so spectacularly successful that they added it to their menu. Since then the tart has gained widespread popularity.

Even novice cooks will be delighted with their success. Our chef stresses the importance of keeping a close watch on the caramel as it cooks. Too dark a caramel often imparts a bitter taste.

For variation, you might use pears instead of apples, or a short pastry instead of puff pastry. But work quickly when you are placing the pastry on top of the apples to prevent it from adhering to the sides of the dish, and put it in the oven immediately.

This beautifully-scented Caramelized Apple Tart is a real classic by any name, and everyone round the table will greet it with delight.

This is the right time to open a bottle of top-quality, farm-produced cider.

3. Place the apple slices in the dish and heat until the butter and sugar form a light caramel. Stir gently from time to time.

4. Meanwhile, roll out the puff pastry and cut out a circle slightly larger than the diameter of the oven-proof dish in which the apples are cooking.

Apple Tart

5. Turn off the heat under the apples as soon as the caramel bubbles up between the apple slices.

6. Lay the circle of puff pastry over top of the apples, turning the overhanging edges in towards the center. Bake in a moderate oven for about 30 minutes.

Pineapple

Ingredients:
2 small pineapples
1 lemon
1¾ cups plus 2 tbsp/
   450 g superfine
   sugar
12 ladyfingers
sugar syrup
1 glass Cointreau
3 egg whites

1. Cut the pineapples in half horizontally. Using a knife and a spoon, scoop out the flesh leaving the rind intact. Place the hollowed-out rinds in the freezer.

Serves 4
Preparation time: 45 minutes
Cooking time: 4 minutes
Difficulty: ✳ ✳

Pineapples originated in the tropical regions of Brazil, the Caribbean, Africa and Asia. In Europe, they could only be grown under glass, and the first French exemplars were presented to King Louis XV. Once costly, today are readily available on the market, especially in winter.

The pineapple is rich in simple sugars and vitamins; according to one theory, they can also help people to lose weight. Be sure to remove the hard, indigestible core.

If the sorbet does not set, it contains too much sugar. In this case, add a little water until the right consistency is reached.

This dessert must be kept in the freezer. Brown the meringue under the grill at the last moment before serving.

Garnished with candied fruits, this dessert becomes a brightly colored feast for the eye as well as the palate. Admittedly, Pineapple Delight is relatively high in calories, but let yourself be tempted, just for once. Serve it at the end of an otherwise light meal.

Our wine expert suggests that you serve small glasses of kirsch or vintage rum.

2. Carefully remove the woody eyes and hard core from the pineapple flesh. Purée the flesh thoroughly in a food processor.

3. Add the juice of the lemon and 1¼ cups/300 g sugar to 2 cups/500 ml of pineapple purée and mix again in the food processor.

4. Transfer the mixture into an ice cream maker and churn until it becomes a sorbet. Fill the frozen pineapple rinds with the sorbet.

Delight

5. Combine the Cointreau with some sugar syrup and soak the ladyfingers with it. Cover the pineapple sorbet with the ladyfingers.

6. Whisk the egg whites into a meringue, adding the rest of the sugar. Using a pastry bag and nozzle, cover the top of the ladyfingers with the meringue and put in the freezer to chill. Just before serving, place under the grill for a few minutes to brown.

Ardennes

1. Warm the milk in a saucepan, then pour it into a large flat pan. Add 3 tbsp/50 g of the sugar to the milk and stir together.

Ingredients:
2 cups/500 ml milk
½ cup plus 2 tbsp/
   150 g superfine
   sugar
2 tbsp vanilla sugar
½ stale baguette,
   sliced
3 whole eggs
6½ tbsp/100 g butter
6½ tbsp/100 ml oil

Serves 4
Preparation time: 15 minutes
Cooking time: 15 minutes
Difficulty: *

2. Stir in the vanilla sugar.

Until recently, bread was regarded as sacred and to waste it was almost a sin. "French toast" was a good way of using up the stale ends of a loaf. Eventually this became a traditional dessert for special occasions in certain regions of France, especially in the south, where it is eaten at Easter, and in the Ardennes.

This dish can be dressed up with the addition of crème anglaise, compote, or fruit preserves thinned with a fruit juice.

This recipe is energy-giving and rich in vitamins A and D and calcium, so it is excellent for children's teeth and bones. A real treat for children, old-fashioned Ardennes French Toast never fails to please. It is quick and simple to make, and always tastes delicious. For an impromptu snack, for informal entertaining, what could be better?

The incomparable mellowness of a Sauternes will add a majestic tone to this unpretentious dessert.

3. Place the bread slices in the milk; turn until well soaked. Separate the eggs and set aside the yolks. Whisk the whites into soft peaks, gradually adding the rest of the sugar.

4. Drain the soaked bread slices on a cake rack. Whisk the egg yolks briskly, then fold them gently into the whites with a wooden spatula.

French Toast

5. Dip the bread slices in the egg mixture, then fry them in a little oil and butter over a low heat, turning from time to time. Remove the slices of French toast from the pan and drain on kitchen paper.

6. When the French toast is well-drained, sprinkle with a little sugar and serve warm.

Exotic

1. Sift the flour into a bowl, then add 1⅔ cups/375 ml of the heavy cream, ½ cup plus 2 tbsp/150 g of the sugar, and the milk. Mix together thoroughly.

Ingredients:
2 generous cups/
   250 g flour
2¾ cups/675 ml
   heavy cream
1 cup plus 2 tbsp/
   280 g sugar
½ cup/125 ml milk
2 eggs, separated
½ package dry yeast
1 kiwi
1 clementine
¼ pineapple
1 mango
1 bunch mint

Serves 6
Preparation time: 15 minutes
Cooking time: 25 minutes
Difficulty: ✵ ✵

2. Lightly whisk in the egg yolks. In another bowl, beat the egg whites with 2 tbsp/30 g sugar until they form soft peaks and set aside.

Waffles have a long history dating back to the ancient Greeks. In the 13th century, a French craftsman forged metal cooking plates with a honeycomb pattern. For a long time, waffles were a staple food of country people; today, they are regarded as one of those delightful extras, appreciated by everyone.

The preparation and serving of waffles reminds many people of childhood, full of nostalgic smells and memories. Children are mad about them—as are grown-ups!

To avoid a lumpy batter, follow the directions strictly: Pour the cold milk and cream into the flour, whisk in the egg yolks lightly, then finally—and this is the secret of producing a light batter—fold in the whisked egg whites. The result is a wonderfully light and airy waffle batter.

The rest is just an enjoyable game of construction. There are no rules for arranging fruit on the waffles—just give your imagination free reign.

Children, of course, will have dozens of ideas of their own for variations: sugared waffles to go with a cuddle; waffles with jam for after school; waffles with crème chantilly for special treats.

To complement this delicacy, serve a fruit juice "cocktail." If adults are joining in the feast, open a bottle of good champagne.

3. Add the yeast, stir briskly, and gently fold in the whisked egg whites with a wooden spatula.

4. Butter the heated waffle iron, then bake the waffles and set them aside.

Fruit Waffles

5. Whisk the remaining cream and sugar into a crème chantilly (see basic recipe) and refrigerate. Just before serving, use a pastry bag fitted with a small nozze to fill each waffle depression with the crème chantilly.

6. Carefully peel the fruits, slice thinly and place on the waffles. Garnish with mint leaves and serve.

Banana and Clementine

Ingredients:
5 bananas
2.2 lbs/1 kg
    clementines
6½ tbsp/100 g sugar
⅔ cup/150 ml sweet
    white wine
2 cups/500 ml crème
    fraîche
¾ cup/180 g butter
10 mint leaves

1. Peel the bananas and slice them slightly on the slant. Brown the slices in butter, drain, and set aside. Peel the clementines, break into segments, and brown in the same pan. Drain and set aside.

Serves 6
Preparation time: 15 minutes
Cooking time: 20 minutes
Difficulty: ✳ ✳

2. Sprinkle the sugar over the bottom of the frying pan and allow it to caramelize.

This is a simple recipe: Just remember to pay attention to the caramel sauce while it is cooking so that it does not become too dark and bitter.

Bananas are very nutritious, advantageous for the bones and for growth in general. Fry the slices gently in butter, and remove them from the pan as soon as they begin to brown to prevent them from softening into a purée! The same is true for the clementines: They need to be just slightly browned.

There is no need to infuse the mint into the sauce because the finely-chopped leaves will release their flavor instantly. The sauce will be a beautiful golden color, setting off the dessert on its dish.

Use crème fraîche or heavy cream for the sauce if possible, since they reduce more quickly. You can also use milk, but cream helps the butter blend smoothly and prevents the possibility of the sauce curdling. For the fruit, you can substitute pears, kiwis, or pineapple and mango.

This fruit-and-cream dessert, sweetly scented, will delight your guests.

Try a little glass of aged rum with it, and success is guaranteed!

3. When the caramel turns an amber color, add the white wine and continue cooking to reduce.

4. After the caramel sauce has reduced to ¾ its initial volume, add the crème fraîche and continue cooking, allowing the sauce to further reduce and thicken.

in Wine Cream

5. Meanwhile, chop the mint leaves very finely and set aside. Stir the butter into the caramel; continue stirring until the sauce has cooled.

6. Just before serving, incorporate the finely chopped mint into the caramel sauce. Arrange the bananas and clementines on a serving dish and cover with sauce.

Wild Strawberry

1. Roll out the puff pastry and, with a pastry cutter, cut out circles about 3 in/7-8 cm in diameter. Arrange them on a baking sheet lined with parchment paper.

Ingredients:
8¾ oz/250 g puff pastry (see basic recipe)
1 quart wild strawberries
6½ tbsp/100 g superfine sugar
1 pint strawberries
⅔ cup/150 g heavy cream
1 cup/150 g confectioners' sugar
mint leaves for decoration
1 cup/250 ml strawberry coulis (see basic recipe)

Serves 4
Preparation time: 20 minutes
Cooking time: 25 minutes
Difficulty: ✶ ✶

Wild strawberries, today rare in nature, have a stronger flavor than the cultivated varieties. If you are not lucky enough to find some in the wild, you can buy *fraises des bois*, or even grow them in your garden. They will be slightly bigger than the truly wild strawberries, with a lovely scarlet color.

This millefeuille is wonderfully luscious and sweet. The puff pastry must be rolled out very thinly to make nice crisp disks. After cutting them out, place the pastry discs in the refrigerator so that they become firm again before facing the heat of the oven. Don't forget to put a second baking sheet on top of the pastry circles; otherwise they will rise too much and make it difficult to assemble the millefeuilles.

Any kind of red fruits can be used in this dessert as long as they are ripe and firm.

Preparing this festive, delightfully scented gâteau is fairly simple, and the results so lavish. Make and serve it to your family as a special treat, a token of love.

Our wine expert recommends a Muscat de Rivesaltes. This superb wine will set the seal on the marvelous marriage of strawberries and puff pastry.

2. Cover the pastry circles with another sheet of parchment paper and place a second baking sheet on top of them to prevent the pastry from rising excessively during baking. Bake in a moderate oven for about 15 minutes.

3. In a blender, make a coulis of the strawberries and superfine sugar (see basic recipe).

4. Strain the coulis to remove all the seeds, then set aside in a cool place. Wash the wild strawberries.

Millefeuille

5. Whisk the cream into a chantilly (see basic recipe), adding half of the confectioners' sugar. When the pastry circles are completely cooled, cover ⅔ of them with the crème chantilly.

6. Arrange the wild strawberries on the cream-covered circles and make double stacks. Cover with a third pastry circle. Sprinkle the rest of the confectioners' sugar over the top; garnish with a wild strawberry and mint leaves. Place on a bed of strawberry coulis and serve with fresh wild strawberries.

Strawberry

1. Whisk the butter in a small bowl until it becomes pale yellow and creamy.

Ingredients:
5½ tbsp/85 g butter
3 eggs
1 lb/500 g
   strawberries
½ cup plus 2 tbsp/
   75 g flour
5 tbsp/75 ml heavy
   cream
1 tbsp superfine
   sugar
1 tsp vanilla extract
mint leaves
⅔ cup/100 g confec-
   tioners' sugar

Serves 4
Preparation time: 15 minutes
Cooking time: 10 minutes
Difficulty: ✶ ✶

2. Separate the eggs. Slightly whisk the yolks and add them to the butter, a little at a time.

If you have a waffle-iron you could make traditionally-shaped waffles, instead of baking them in molds in the oven.

Add the egg yolks to the batter one at a time to obtain a well-blended mixture. The flour and whisked egg whites must be added to the butter and egg yolk mixture at the same time. This will give the batter a rather odd appearance, as though it had curdled, but don't be alarmed: It is supposed to look rather grainy before going into the oven.

The waffles will be crisper if you use a waffle iron, but our chef assures us that baking the batter in individual shallow molds will also produce good results.

Sweet or savory, waffles are always a real treat. In the past, together with crêpes, they were one of the staples of people's diets in the rural areas of France. Today they are sold on street corners. You can revive an old tradition and delight your children and friends by making these delicious Strawberry Waffles, whatever the season.

Our wine expert suggests the cheerful color of a Champagne Veuve Clicquot rosé to accompany this sweet treat.

3. Whisk the egg whites into soft peaks. Use the strawberries to prepare a strawberry coulis (see basic recipe), reserving a few for the garnish.

4. Gradually add the sifted flour together with the whisked egg whites to the butter and egg yolk mixture.

Waffles

5. Whisk the heavy cream into a chantilly (see basic recipe), adding the sugar toward the end. Gently fold the crème chantilly into the egg mixture and add a few drops of vanilla extract.

6. Generously butter individual forms and fill with the waffle mixture. Smooth the surface, then bake in the oven for 5–6 minutes. Turn out the waffles and sprinkle with confectioners' sugar. Garnish with mint leaves and serve accompanied by the strawberry coulis.

Cheese Bavarois

1. Add a few drops of vanilla extract to a little water in a saucepan. Dissolve the gelatin in cold water, then add to the water and vanilla, and heat.

Ingredients:
vanilla extract
4 leaves gelatin
8¾ oz/250 g cream cheese
1 cup/250 ml heavy cream
4 tbsp sugar
8¾ oz/250 g strawberries
8¾ oz/250 g red currants
8¾ oz/250 g raspberries

Serves 6
Preparation time: 15 minutes
Chilling time: 4 hours
Difficulty: ✳

2. Remove the vanilla mixture from the heat. Stir in the cream cheese, whisk vigorously and set aside.

A *bavarois* is a light and yet rich cream set with gelatin. The novelty in this recipe is the use of cream cheese instead of the more traditional custard component. The cream is certain to set properly as long as the crème chantilly is cold before folding it into the cheese and gelatin mixture.

Dissolve the gelatin well in cold water before adding it to the vanilla syrup in order to eliminate its rather acrid taste. The gelatin's function is to make the bavarois set, not to affect its flavor. Just dip the bottom of the mold in hot water to ease turning the bavarois out onto the serving platter.

This is a delightful dessert with which to end any kind of meal, even the heartiest, on a light note. If you are making this dessert for adults, strawberry or raspberry brandy can be added instead of vanilla for flavoring. But the bavarois does not keep well, so it must be served the same day it is made.

Our wine expert suggests serving a Muscat de Beaumes-de-Venise with the Cheese Bavarois with Red Berries. The special fruitiness of this wine will complement the bavarois perfectly.

3. Whisk the heavy cream into a crème chantilly with the sugar (see basic recipe). Wash the fruit and cut the strawberries into small pieces.

4. When the cheese mixture has cooled, add it to the crème chantilly, folding it in gently.

with Red Berries

5. Add the fruit to this preparation and gently stir.

6. Fill a mold and place it in the refrigerator for 3 or 4 hours to set. Turn out of the mold just before serving with a raspberry coulis (see basic recipe).

Ingredients:
2 cups/500 ml water
10 tbsp/150 g butter
pinch salt
3⅓ cups/400 g flour
15 eggs
zest of 1 lemon
6½ tbsp/100 ml kirsch
9 tbsp/200 g apricot
   preserves
oil for frying
confectioners' sugar
   for dusting

1. Prepare a choux pastry with the water, butter, salt and flour (see basic recipe).

Serves 6
Preparation time: 15 minutes
Cooking time: 45 minutes
Difficulty: ✳ ✳

2. Remove the pan from the heat and add the whole eggs one at a time, stirring vigorously so that they do not cook.

Pets-de-nonne, or "nun's farts," is certainly a surprising name for a pastry. According to legend, a bishop was once visiting a convent kitchen where a young nun was busy preparing fritters. Flustered at the arrival of this important visitor, she made an unfortunate little noise. The bishop, who was known to have a sense of humor, asked the mother superior the name of this dish. The quick-witted mother replied: "They are *pets-de-nonne*, Monsignor!" And that is how this classic *pâtisserie* acquired its rather indelicate name.

Our chef reminds us that the oil should be very hot before dropping the fritters into it. Once they are cooking you can lower the heat. Turn them continually with a slotted spoon. When they have swelled up, turn up the heat again to brown their exterior and stop the expansion.

This airy dessert is known as *chichi* in Provence, where it is traditionally eaten during Mardi Gras. But there is no need to wait for the Carnival season to make these marvelous little fritters, especially for any deserving children you know, who will devour them with enthusiasm at any time of year.

It is worth opening a great champagne—a Veuve Clicquot Grande Dame, for example—to drink with this dessert.

3. Grate the lemon zest into the choux pastry and stir again.

4. Add 3½ tbsp/50 ml of the kirsch and blend it in.

de-Nonne

5. For the coulis, combine the apricot preserves, the rest of the kirsch, and 1 tbsp confectioners' sugar in a blender and mix thoroughly.

6. Heat the oil and use 2 spoons to form small fritters from the choux pastry; fry them. Serve hot, sprinkled with confectioners' sugar and accompanied by the apricot coulis.

Iced Grand

1. For the génoise, thoroughly beat the whole eggs and 3 tbsp/50 g superfine sugar together to the ribbon stage. Add the potato flour and ground almonds. Whisk the egg whites into soft peaks with the rest of the sugar and gently fold into the first mixture.

2. Butter a piece of parchment paper and place on baking sheet. With a spatula, spread the génoise mixture to a depth of about ⅜ in/1 cm. Bake in a moderate oven for about 15 minutes.

3. Cut the génoise into 4 rectangles. Spread red currant jelly on each piece, then stack them and cut into slices about ⅜ in/1 cm thick. Line a charlotte form or other mold with the slices, pressing them against the sides.

Ingredients:
6½ tbsp/100 g superfine sugar
6 egg yolks
3 egg whites
1 cup/250 ml heavy cream
6½ tbsp/100 ml Grand Marnier
chocolate sauce (see basic recipe)
For the génoise:
4½ tbsp/70 g superfine sugar
2 eggs; 3 egg whites
½ cup/60 g potato flour
1½ tbsp/20 g ground almonds
½ cup/180 g red currant jelly

Serves 8
Preparation time: 40 minutes
Cooking time: 15 minutes
Freezing time: 4–5 hours
Difficulty: ✶ ✶

For anyone with a busy schedule, this is just the right recipe. This charlotte can be made a day in advance, which may allow you a little time for yourself before the guests arrive. In order to avoid a grainy texture, whisk the eggs whites just until they start to become firm, add the sugar, and then complete the whisking. Cut the génoise while it is still hot because it very quickly hardens and then breaks easily.

While the mousse is freezing, prepare the chocolate sauce according to the basic recipe. Make it with unsweetened cocoa, and add sugar according to your own taste. Serve the chocolate sauce hot, and savor the delicious contrast between the hot sauce and ice-cold mousse filling of the charlotte.

To complete this pleasurable experience, serve your guests a little glass of Grand Marnier, or else a sparkling Champagne Veuve Clicquot.

4. For the mousse filling, beat half the sugar with the 6 egg yolks. Whisk the egg whites into soft peaks with the remaining sugar. Gently fold the egg whites into the egg yolks.

Marnier Charlotte

5. Blend in the Grand Marnier. Whisk the cream into a chantilly, fold into the egg mixture, and gently combine.

6. Fill the mold with the Grand Marnier mousse and place it in a freezer for 4–5 hours to harden. Turn out of the mold, garnish with orange slices, and serve with a hot chocolate sauce (see basic recipe).

Floating Islands

1. To make the syrup, bring the water to a boil and stir in the sugar.

Ingredients:

For the syrup:
4 cups/1 liter water
¼ cup/60 g sugar
1 vanilla bean

For the raspberry coulis:
14 oz/400 g raspberries
6½ tbsp/100 g sugar
juice of 1 lemon

For the floating islands:
4 egg whites
¼ cup/60 g sugar
pinch salt
1¼ cups/300 ml vanilla
  ice cream
1 bunch mint

Serves 4
Preparation time: 20 minutes
Cooking time: 10 minutes
Difficulty: ☆ ☆

2. Split the vanilla bean, steep it in the syrup for 15 minutes, then remove.

This recipe is a new version of a classic dessert, and these glistening meringue islands floating on a sea of juicy red raspberry coulis are more irresistible than ever!

Our chef recommends adding the sugar to the egg whites in three stages, to prevent them from becoming grainy.

Poach the whisked egg-white "islands" in barely simmering syrup. If it starts to boil, the egg whites will swell up too quickly and then immediately deflate. So cook them very gently to ensure a beautifully puffed-up meringue.

A useful tip: The egg whites will slip off the ladle easily if you dip it in the syrup each time before scooping out a portion. This will also help to form the meringue into nice round shapes, which will look all the more impressive on the serving dish.

If you are in the mood for innovation, why not try floating your islands on a dramatic dark velvet bed of black currant or blueberry coulis? If the coulis seems too thick (depending on the kind of fruit used), it can be thinned with a little syrup. Do not be afraid to introduce your more traditionally-minded friends to this unabashed novelty— they will be grateful after they have tried it.

Nothing would enhance these beautiful Floating Islands with Raspberry Coulis better than a Champagne Veuve Clicquot brut.

3. For the coulis, purée most of the raspberries in an electric blender, reserving a few berries to garnish. Add the sugar and lemon juice to the purée and blend. Press the coulis through a fine sieve.

4. For the "islands," whisk the egg whites into soft peaks, add the sugar and a pinch of salt, and continue whisking until very stiff.

with Raspberry Coulis

5. Heat the syrup again. Ladle out smoothly rounded portions of meringue and slide them into the syrup. Poach for a few minutes, turning them from time to time. When they are done, remove from the syrup and drain on a sheet of paper towel.

6. Pour the raspberry coulis onto a serving dish and carefully arrange the floating islands on top. Place a ball of vanilla ice cream on the center of each meringue, garnish with raspberries and mint leaves, and serve immediately.

Glazed

1. Prepare a crème anglaise with the ingredients listed; follow the basic recipe but infuse the milk with the vanilla bean instead of adding vanilla extract. Dissolve the gelatin in cold water, then add it to ¾ of the crème anglaise, reserving the rest.

Ingredients:
8 egg yolks
6½ tbsp/100 g
    superfine sugar
4 cups/1 liter milk
1 vanilla bean
8 leaves gelatin
6 oz/175 g
    sweetened
    chestnut purée
2½ tbsp/40 ml
    Cognac
5 tbsp glazed
    chestnut pieces
2 tbsp/30 g heavy
    cream

Serves 6
Preparation time: 25 minutes
Cooking time: 5 minutes
Chilling time: 4–6 hours
Difficulty: ✶ ✶

Fans of chesnuts cannot fail but be delighted by our chef's recipe—and you will indeed be delighted by its simplicity and exquisite texture.

Chestnut trees thrive in Alsace, where numerous regional dished based on these nutritous nuts add a bit of warmth to the raw, icy days of winter. Chestnuts contain calcium, folic acid, potassium, and magnesium and are generally good for your health.

When you mix the crème anglaise with the chestnut purée, whisk them well to prevent lumps from forming. The crème chantilly, on the other hand, must be folded in very gently with a wooden spatula using delicate, light strokes.

A few drops of Cognac will give a pleasant flavor to the crème anglaise reserved for covering the bottom of the serving dish.

Glazed Chestnut Delight can be made at any time of year because, unlike fresh chestnuts, canned glazed chestnuts are always available. The dessert should always be served very cold, but it can be enjoyed in winter just as much as in summer.

Our wine expert suggests drinking a Champagne Veuve Clicquot Carte Jaune.

2. Whisk the crème anglaise and gelatin until the gelatin has dissolved, and allow to cool. Add the sweet chestnut puree and whisk very vigorously.

3. And the Cognac to the chestnut mixture.

4. Incorporate the glazed chestnuts pieces.

Chestnut Delight

5. Whisk the heavy cream into a chantilly (see basic recipe), then fold it into the chestnut cream.

6. Pour the mixture into a mold and place in the refrigerator for 4–6 hours. Serve with the reserved crème anglaise, into which a few drops of Cognac have been blended.

Caramelized Pears

1. Peel the pears, but do not remove the stems. Rub with half a lemon to prevent discoloring and set aside.

Ingredients:
4 Williams pears
1 lemon
2 cups/500 ml water
3¾ cups/900 g sugar
1 vanilla bean
1 tbsp butter
1¾ oz/50 g pistachios
2 cups/500 ml vanilla
   ice cream
sprigs of mint

Serves 4
Preparation time: 10 minutes
Cooking time: 30 minutes
Difficulty: ✴

2. In a large saucepan, bring the water to a boil. Add half of the sugar and the vanilla bean, slit lengthwise, and cook to obtain a syrup.

This dessert will give your table a festive appearance. It is easy to make, and you will have fun decorating the pears with pistachios.

Choose pears with firm flesh; our chef prefers Williams pears. To prevent them from discoloring, add the juice of half a lemon to the syrup in which they are poached.

The caramel must not stick to the plates, nor harden to toffee. For a perfect caramel, carefully add up to half a glass of water once it has reached the right color to stop it from cooking any further and make it slightly more liquid. If you pour in the water too quickly, the caramel will spatter dangerously. Heed this warning!

This simple, elegant dessert is appropriate for all kinds of occasion: for family dinners, celebrations with friends, or formal entertaining.

Our wine expert says that a pear liqueur is the obvious choice here. Produced mainly by distilleries in the Loire, it is very appealing—especially to women, so they say....

3. Reserve 1 tbsp sugar then pour the rest of the sugar into another saucepan. Add some water and heat to produce a caramel. As soon as it turns a nice amber color, halt the cooking process by adding a little water while stirring constantly. Allow to cool.

4. Poach the pears in the syrup made in Step 2 for about 15 minutes.

with Vanilla Ice Cream

5. Remove and drain the pears. Sauté them gently in the butter and reserved 1 tbsp sugar until they turn a golden brown color.

6. Pour a little of the cold caramel onto each dessert plate. In the center of each plate, place a pear studded with pistachios. Arrange small spoonfuls of vanilla ice cream around the pears, garnish with mint, and serve.

Yema

1. For the praline, heat ½ cup plus 2 tbsp/150 sugar and the lemon juice until a golden-brown caramel is formed, then add the flaked almonds. Mix well and cook until the almonds are well-browned. Stir in the butter and pour the praline onto an oiled baking sheet to cool.

2. Separate the eggs and place the yolks in a large saucepan. Add the rest of the sugar and whisk together vigorously over very low heat until it becomes a pale, almost white, cream.

3. Break up the cooled praline and add to half of the egg yolk mixture; reserve the rest.

Ingredients:
1 cup/250 g sugar
juice of 1 lemon
2 cups/200 g flaked
 almonds
3½ tbsp/50 g butter
6 eggs
1 cup/250 ml heavy
 cream
1 génoise
 (see basic recipe)
1 cup/250 ml pastry
 cream (see basic
 recipe)
confectioners' sugar

Serves 8
Preparation time: 40 minutes
Cooking time: 10 minutes
Freezing time: 3 hours
Difficulty: ✳ ✳ ✳

This gâteau takes rather a long time to prepare, but the result is sensational! It does freeze well, and can be made several days in advance. If desired, you can save yourself one step and buy a ready-made génoise.

Be careful not to overcook the caramel when making the praline. Remove it from the heat as soon as the caramel turns reddish-brown, otherwise it will become bitter and spoil the flavor of the entire gâteau.

Although this recipe requires several different components—pastry cream, crème chantilly, and praline—don't panic. Just be sure to allow yourself enough time. Start preparing the dessert a day or two in advance. This marvelous Yema Gâteau is worth all the time and effort it takes! You can serve it at the end of any kind of festive meal, and it will win you compliments all around.

In the opinion of our wine expert, a very good Champagne brut Henriot is a perfect complement to the crunchiness of the nougat.

4. Whisk the heavy cream into an unsweetened crème chantilly (see basic recipe), and fold it gently into the praline mixture.

Gâteau

5. Slice the génoise horizontally into 2 layers; place one half in the bottom of a cake ring. Fill the mold ¾ full with the praline cream, and cover with the second layer of génoise.

6. Thoroughly combine the pastry cream with the reserved egg yolk mixture, and fill the cake ring with it. Sprinkle generously with confectioners' sugar and caramelize the surface under the broiler or with a blowtorch. Freeze for 3 hours before removing the cake ring and serving.

Apricot

1. Bring 1 cup/250 ml milk to a boil in a saucepan, add the sugar, and sprinkle in the semolina while whisking vigorously. Allow to cool.

Ingredients:
1½ cups/350 ml milk
3½ tbsp/50 g sugar
½ cup plus 1 tbsp/
    70 g fine wheat
    semolina
4 leaves gelatin
⅔ cup/150 ml heavy
    cream
8 apricot halves

Serves 4
Preparation time: 10 minutes
Cooking time: 10 minutes
Chilling time: 2 hours
Difficulty: ✲

Poached eggs on a plate for dessert? Your guests may look rather perturbed when you serve this dessert at the end of the meal, but any children children present are likely to enjoy the joke.

Allow the cooked semolina to cool well before combining it with the crème chantilly.

This is a very light dish, and very easy to prepare. It can also be made in advance because it will keep for two to three days in the refrigerator; it needs to be chilled for at least two hours before serving.

As well as being amusing, it is also good for you. The "egg white" is rich in calcium; the "yolk" in iron and vitamins A, B1 and B2. Serve Apricot "Eggs" at informal meals to friends who like laughing as well as eating.

To add to the enjoyment, our wine expert suggests a Quarts de Chaume: This great but little-known wine, with its peach-and-apricot flavors, will be a perfect accent.

2. Dissolve the gelatin in cold water. Heat the remaining milk in a saucepan and whisk in the gelatin briskly.

3. Add in the semolina mixture and stir energetically to combine.

4. Whisk the heavy cream into a chantilly (see basic recipe) and fold it into the cooled semolina mixture. Gently stir to aerate.

"Eggs"

5. Put 2–3 tbsp of the mixture into individual shallow gratin dishes. Tap the bottom of each dish so that the mixture spreads to cover the surface.

6. In the center of each dish arrange 2 apricot halves to give the appearance of poached eggs on a plate. Place in the refrigerator and serve well-chilled.

Lemon

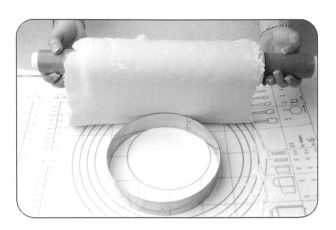

1. Prepare a sweet short pastry according to the recipe, roll it out, and use it to line a fairly deep cake ring. Prick the base lightly with a fork.

Ingredients:
10½ oz/300 g sweet
  short pastry
  (see basic recipe
  for short pastry)
1 cup/250 ml pastry
  cream (see basic
  recipe)
2 lemons
3½ tbsp/50 ml kirsch
8 egg whites
4½ tbsp/70 g sugar

Serves 6
Preparation time: 25 minutes
Cooking time: 40 minutes
Difficulty: ✳ ✳

2. Spread a layer of the pastry cream over the bottom.

This is a dessert to be savored without the least feeling of guilt: It is low in calories, high in vitamin C, and the acidity of the lemon lends it a light, rather than rich, quality.

The secret of the soufflé lies in the correct preparation of the meringue mixture. To make sure the meringue is perfect, the chef recommends adding a pinch of salt to the egg whites before whisking them, and then sprinkling in the sugar while continuing to whisk. The meringue should be firm, but not too dry.

If you prefer, you could make an Orange Soufflé Tart by substituting oranges for the lemons, and Grand Marnier for the kirsch.

This beautiful Lemon Soufflé Tart will not let you down in front of your guests: It will not collapse miserably as some soufflés tend to do if they are kept waiting, and it is not at all sweet, making it a pleasant end to any kind of meal.

To set off the acidity of the lemon and the softness of the meringue, our wine expert recommends a Champagne brut Veuve Clicquot.

3. Grate the lemon zest and peel the lemons. Cut the fruit into wedges and arrange them on the pastry cream. Bake the tart for 20 minutes.

4. Add the lemon zest and kirsch to the rest of the pastry cream and stir to combine.

Soufflé Tart

5. Whisk the egg whites until very stiff, adding the sugar gradually. Fold them gently into the pastry cream.

6. Spoon the meringue onto the tart to a height of about 2¾ in/7 cm and carefully smooth its surface. Bake in a moderate oven for about 20 minutes, dust the top with confectioners's sugar, and serve warm.

Almond and Melon

1. Separate the eggs. Add half of the confectioners' sugar to the egg whites and whisk until they are very stiff. Add the other half of the sugar to the crème fraîche and whip.

2. Gently blend the sweetened crème fraîche and the beaten egg whites.

Ingredients:
4 eggs
2 cups/300 g confectioners' sugar
2 cups/500 ml crème fraîche
1¼ cups/125 g flaked almonds
6½ tbsp/75 g candied orange peel
5 tbsp melon sorbet
1 sheet aluminum foil
raspberry coulis
whole raspberries and figs to garnish

Serves 6
Preparation time: 25 minutes
Cooking time: 5 minutes
Chilling time: 6 hours
Difficulty: ✶

This luscious almond ice cream is deliciously crunchy, and you will lose your heart to its delicate sweetness.

Originally from Asia, almonds were very popular with the Romans; and, in the Middle Ages, the knights and ladies enjoyed eating them both in soups and sweet dishes. Almonds contain sugar, protein, oil, and myriad vitamns and minerals. When dried, they are even richer in protein, fat, and sugar.

For optimal results, our chef advises whisking the egg whites with confectioners' sugar. He also recommends sweetening the coulis just enough so that it is not tart, so that its flavor does not drown that of the iced nougat. If you do not have an ice cream maker, you can of course buy the sorbet ready-made.

This cooling and colorful dessert will gain pride of place on your table in summer.

Contrary to what is often believed, a Sauterne is not always the best wine to accompany desserts. But when sweetened almonds are used, as here, it is the best possible choice. Our wine expert recommends a Château Bêchereau.

3. Roast the almonds under a grill, leave them to cool, then gently fold them into the mixture.

4. Cut the candied orange peel into cubes and add it to the nougat mixture.

Nougat Glacé

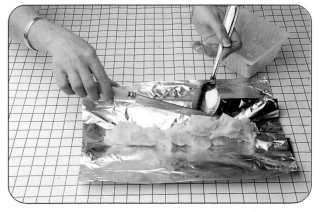

5. Place the melon sorbet on a piece of aluminum foil, wrap it up to form a roll, and freeze.

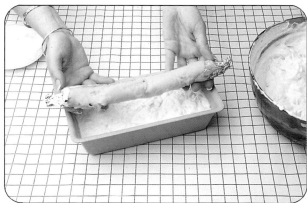

6. Turn half of the nougat mixture into a loaf pan, place the roll of melon sorbet in the center, and top with the rest of the nougat. Chill for 5–6 hours. To serve, cut the nougat into slices and garnish with raspberry coulis, whole raspberries, and figs.

Crème

1. Bring the milk to a boil, and grate the zest of the lime into it.

Ingredients:
4 cups/1 liter milk
1 lime
1 pinch cinnamon
3 whole eggs
3 egg yolks
⅓ cup/40 g cornstarch
1¼ cups/300 g sugar

Serves 6
Preparation time: 10 minutes
Cooking time: 10 minutes
Difficulty: ✳

2. Sprinkle the cinnamon into the milk and cook over gentle heat just until the first bubbles appear.

The south of Catalonia, with its bright sunlight and lovely language, is our chef's inspiration for this delicious dessert.

Our chef recommends that you do not let the custard boil. As soon as the first bubble appears, pour the mixture quickly into the form. This is important to prevent the custard from curdling. It is best to make it a day in advance so that it is thoroughly chilled when it is time to caramelize the sugar.

A cast iron blini pan, small and round, can be used to glaze the top of the dessert. If you do not have one, you can use the base of any small cast iron saucepan.

Star anise or fennel seed both have flavors marvellously suited to this dessert, and can be used instead of cinnamon. Serve the Crème Catalan chilled, but do not refrigerate it after caramelizing the sugar, or you will destroy the character of the dish.

Satisfying and quick to make, this dessert deserves to be prepared more often.

Our wine expert recommends a dry sherry.

3. Break the eggs into a bowl. Add the egg yolks, cornstarch, and ¾ cup plus 1 tbsp/200 g of the sugar and stir vigorously with a whisk.

4. Pour the boiling milk into the egg mixture while stirring vigorously. Pour into a saucepan and cook as for a crème anglaise (see basic recipe).

Catalan

5. Pour the custard thus obtained into a dish and place in the refrigerator.

6. Just before serving, sprinkle the rest of the sugar over the chilled Crème Catalan. Place a cast iron pan in the oven and heat until white-hot, then move it carefully above the surface to caramelize the sugar. Garnish as desired and serve.

Pears on Puff Pastry

1. Carefully peel the pears, leaving their stems intact. Fill a large saucepan with water and bring to a boil. Dissolve the sugar in it and poach the pears in this syrup. Allow to cool in the syrup.

Ingredients:
4 medium-sized pears
1 cup/250 g sugar
1 lb/500 g puff pastry
  (see basic recipe)
For the pastry cream:
3½ tbsp/50 g sugar
¼ cup/30 g flour
3 egg yolks
1¼ cups/300 ml milk
For the caramel:
1 cup/250 g sugar
1 cup/250 ml crème
  fraîche
fresh mint leaves for
  decoration

Serves 4
Preparation time: 30 minutes
Cooking time: 45 minutes
Difficulty: ✶ ✶

2. For the pastry cream, combine the sugar, flour and the egg yolks and stir together vigorously. Bring the milk to a boil in a saucepan.

For this recipe, our chef recommends using a firm pear that will stand up to cooking. Alternatively, you might use apples or peaches. Simply adapt the recipe according to the time of year and the availability of fruit.

To retain the pears' pale color, rub them thoroughly with a half lemon as soon as they are peeled. But our chef reminds you not to overcook the fruit; keep in mind that the pears will continue cooking as long as the syrup is warm. To test whether they are done, insert the point of a knife into the flesh: You should still feel a little resistance.

Serve this dessert hot with a cold caramel sauce. The contrast between hot and cold, and between melting and crisp textures, is absolutely delicious. You may find that people are continually asking you to make it.

Fruit brandies go very well with desserts because the concentration of alcohol subtly counteracts out any over-sweetness. Our wine expert suggests a little glass of iced pear brandy. And for the children, why not a glass of cold water!

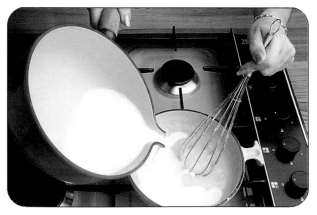

3. Pour the boiling milk on the egg yolk mixture, whisk vigorously, and pour back into the saucepan. Cook over very low heat, stirring continuously. Allow to boil for a few seconds, then remove from the heat and pour into another receptacle.

4. Roll out the puff pastry and cut out 4 pieces in the shape of a pear. Prick them lightly with a fork, then place a spoonful of pastry cream on each.

with Caramel Sauce

5. Halve the cooled poached pears and remove their seeds. Slice the pears thinly and arrange in fans on the pastry cream. Bake in a moderate oven for about 20 minutes.

6. For the caramel sauce, heat the sugar until it turns a light brown color. Stir in the crème fraîche and continue cooking for 2–3 minutes. Remove from the heat and allow to cool. Serve with the pear pastries. If desired, garnish with mint leaves.

Chestnut

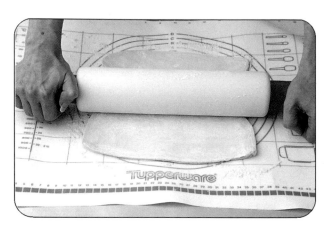

1. Cut the puff pastry into 3 pieces. Roll each of them out with a rolling pin.

Ingredients:
12¾ oz/350 g puff pastry (see basic recipe)
8¾ oz/250 g vanilla-flavored chestnut purée
6½ tbsp/100 g butter
2 tbsp/30 ml aged rum
6½ tbsp/100 ml heavy cream
3½ oz/100 g glazed chestnuts
⅔ cup/100 g confectioners' sugar

Serves 6
Preparation time: 15 minutes
Cooking time: 20 minutes
Difficulty: ✲✲

2. Cut an approximately 7¾-in/20-cm square out of each sheet of pastry.

For nearly a century, the delicate cream-filled stack of puff pastry know as *millefeuille* has been one of the best-known and most popular of all pastries, and it lends itself to many versions. This one has a filling based on chestnut purée and glazed chestnuts.

Sugar-glazed chestnuts, or *marrons glacés*, are a gourmet sweetmeat dating back to the time of Louis XIV, and their preparation requires a great deal of care and patience. This dessert is not difficult to prepare if you can find ready-made glazed chestnuts and chestnut purée. If your purée is sweetened, however, do not add sugar to the crème chantilly. When you have combined the butter and chestnut purée, fold in the crème chantilly, and do not beat the mixture further.

Our chef points out that although rum is traditionally used in conjunction with chestnuts, if you fancy a change, you could use whisky instead. This hint of Scotland will produce a pleasantly novel effect. Another variation substitutes a purée of prunes for the chestnuts; in this case, the rum should be replaced by Armagnac.

Serve Glazed Chestnut Millefeuille very well chilled, dusted with confectioners' sugar, and lovingly decorated with a few whole glazed chestnuts and one or two mint leaves.

Our wine expert would like to take this opportunity to recommend a great sweet wine, Maury, with its mingled notes of cocoa and prune.

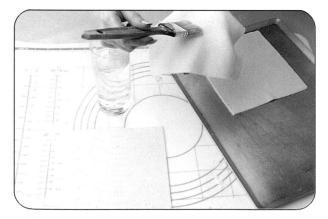

3. Moisten the squares with water, using a pastry brush. Place on a baking sheet and bake in a medium-hot oven until golden brown.

4. Mix the chestnut purée with the butter, blending thoroughly with an electric mixer.

Millefeuille

5. Stir the rum into the purée. Whisk the heavy cream with half the confectioners' sugar into a chantilly (see basic recipe). Gently fold the whipped cream into the chestnut purée mixture.

6. Spread a layer of the chestnut filling on 2 of the puff pastry squares. Coarsely chop the glazed chestnuts and sprinkle over the filling. Layer the squares with the filling and top with the third piece of pastry. Dust with confectioners' sugar and serve well-chilled.

Morello Cherry

Ingredients:
1 cup/250 ml white wine
6½ tbsp/100 g superfine sugar
1¼ cups/300 ml crème fraîche
3 egg yolks
3½ tbsp/50 ml kirsch
5¼ oz/150 g Morello cherries

Serves 6
Preparation time: 25 minutes
Cooking time: 10 minutes
Freezing time: 3 hours
Difficulty: ✳

1. Combine the white wine and sugar in a saucepan, bring to a boil, and reduce to a very thick syrup. Allow to cool somewhat.

People who take desserts seriously know that they can be eaten at any time of day, any time of year. Not only do provide a delightful end to a meal, but we can also enjoy them as snacks in between meals!

In place of the wine, you might choose a Gewürztraminer or even a good champagne to make the syrup. For a perfect mousse, whisk the egg yolks until they are frothy, and wait until the syrup has cooled a bit before adding it to the beaten egg yolks. Continue whisking very vigorously to prevent the eggs from cooking and turning lumpy. The cream must be whisked until it is quite stiff and folded into the egg and syrup mixture with a wooden spatula, using a high, circular movement.

Use kirsch to flavor the mousse if you enjoy the flavor of alcohol in a dessert, or the juice from preserved cherries to make it sweeter and alcohol-free. Reserve a few whole Morello cherries, with their stalks, to garnish. This light and airy dessert, served frozen, will delight even those who claim they are not very hungry.

Our wine expert recommends that you serve each guest a little glass of chilled cherry brandy, the obvious choice to drink with the splended Morello Cherry Mousse Glacé.

2. In a bowl resting on ice cubes, whisk the crème fraîche into a crème chantilly (see basic recipe).

3. Place the egg yolks in a large bowl. When the thick wine syrup is lukewarm, whisk it into the egg yolks a little at a time. Continue whisking until completely cool.

4. Gently fold the chantilly cream into the egg yolk and wine syrup mixture.

Mousse Glacé

5. Add the kirsch and stir gently again.

6. Remove the stalks and stones from the cherries. Gently stir the cherries into the cream mixture and place in the freezer for 3 hours to harden. Garnish and serve frozen.

Crêpes with Orange and

1. Stir half of the Grand Marnier into the pastry cream and whisk vigorously over very low heat to produce a warm and very smooth mixture.

Ingredients:
8 crêpes
   (see basic recipe)
⅓ cup/80 ml Grand
   Marnier
2 cups/500 ml pastry
   cream (see basic
   recipe)
½ cup plus 2 tbsp/
   150 g sugar
3½ tbsp/50 g butter
2 oranges
3½ tbsp/50 g
   superfine sugar for
   topping

Serves 4
Preparation time: 15 minutes
Cooking time: 10 minutes
Difficulty: ✶ ✶

2. Spread a thin layer of the Grand Marnier-flavored pastry cream over each crêpe. Fold them twice to form wedges and set aside.

Everyone, young and old, adores crêpes, so why wait for a special occasion to make them? Here is a recipe for crêpes that are unusual enough to arouse interest, but familiar enough to please everyone.

Oranges must be the mythical golden apples in the garden of the Hesperides. When you tell this story to children, they will be keen to help you in this little labor of Hercules....

One piece of advice which will help you produce a successful pastry cream: Patiently beat the egg yolk and sugar mixture until it is frothy and pale before adding the flour. During the whole time the pastry cream is cooking, whisking very vigorously to prevent the mixture from sticking to the bottom of the pan.

If you want to light up your dinner party, these crêpes can be flambéed with Grand Marnier which, of course, is a liqueur based on orange and Cognac.

And to drink, our wine expert suggests either fresh orange juice, Grand Marnier, or a Veuve Clicquot Champagne: The choice is yours.

3. Pour the sugar into a saucêpan and heat it to produce a caramel.

4. When the caramel turns golden brown, add the butter and stir well.

Grand Marnier Coulis

5. Squeeze the oranges and pour the juice into the caramel mixture; heat for a few moments. Arrange the crêpes on an ovenproof serving dish.

6. Pour the rest of the Grand Marnier into the caramel sauce and continue heating for a few seconds. Cover the crêpes with the sauce and sprinkle with superfine sugar. Place in the oven for 5–6 minutes at medium heat, and serve.

Peaches in

1. Bring the water to a boil, then add the wine, chopped vanilla bean, thyme and sugar. Cook over moderate heat for 15 minutes. Allow to cool.

Ingredients:
2 cups/500 ml water
1 cup/250 ml
    Sauternes wine
1 vanilla bean, finely
    chopped
3 springs thyme
2 cups/500 g sugar
6 peaches
1 bundle rhubarb,
    about 1 lb
1 bunch mint

Serves 6
Preparation time: 20 minutes
Cooking time: 30 minutes
Chilling time: 2 hours
Difficulty: ✶

2. When the syrup has cooled, add the whole peaches, cover the pan, and cook over a very low heat.

The English first adapted rhubarb to cooking, especially in rhubarb pies. Before the 18th century it had been regarded as a medicinal or ornamental plant, and today it is used mainly to make jams or compotes. Fresh rhubarb is available from May to July.

Rhubarb is low in calories, and contains phosphorous, potassium, magnesium, iron and vitamins. The leaves, with their oxalic acid, are extremely laxative and not to be eaten. The chef offers several pieces of advice: Wait for the syrup to cool before adding the peaches and, later, the rhubarb. Poach the peaches in simmering—hot boiling—syrup, and be sure to cover the pot. Remove the peaches, thyme and chopped vanilla bean from the syrup when the peaches are cooked, and reduce the syrup. Poach the rhubarb very slowly, because it overcooks very easily and turns into compote.

Make Peaches in Rhubarb Sauce the day before it is needed; in fact, it will keep for several days in the refrigerator. Serve it well-chilled. Its delightful fragrance is very refreshing on a hot summer's day.

Our wine expert recommends a Quarts de Chaume here. The color, sweetness and charm of this great but too little-known wine will be a marvelous accompaniment to this summery dessert.

3. Remove the leaves from the rhubarb and peel away the stringy fibers.

4. Cut the rhubarb into short pieces. Remove the peaches from the syrup and set aside. Continue cooking until the syrup is reduced by ¼, then allow to cool.

Rhubarb Sauce

5. Add the rhubarb to the reduced syrup, bring to a boil, cook for a few moments, and remove from the heat. Temporarily remove the rhubarb from the syrup (so that it does not continue to cook) and leave to cool.

6. Carefully peel the peaches and arrange on a serving dish accompanied by the rhubarb in syrup. Garnish with chopped mint leaves and serve well-chilled.

1. Whisk the butter and confectioners' sugar vigorously together with the vanilla extract.

Ingredients:
For the shells:
5 tbsp/75 g butter
½ cup/75 g confec-
    tioners' sugar
1 tsp/5 ml vanilla
    extract
½ cup plus 2 tbsp/
    75 g flour
1 egg white
14 oz/400 g wild
    strawberries (*fraise
    des bois*)
1 bunch mint
raspberry coulis
    (see basic recipe)
1 tbsp honey

Serves 4
Preparation time: 20 minutes
Cooking time: 5 minutes
Difficulty: ✴ ✴ ✴

2. Add the egg white to this mixture and whisk until well-blended.

The little strawberries that are found in the wild in June, at lower altitudes in July, and in the mountains in August and September, easily surpass all the cultivated varieties in both scent and flavor. A taste of these pretty little fruits is an unforgettable pleasure.

Strawberries are low in calories and their sugar is easily assimilated, making them an ideal treat for diabetics.

Our chef advises you to lift the pastry from the baking sheet very delicately using a spatula. Do this immediately after removing them from the oven while the pastry is still soft and flexible. Because it is so thin it cools quickly, and will break when you lay it over the base of the bowl. In order to achieve successful "tulips," you must mix the ingredients in the exact order given (see also the basic recipe for *pâte à tuile*).

This delicious, refreshing dessert, with its pretty shape of an open flower, will provide a stylish finish to your summer meals.

Our wine expert suggests a Champagne Veuve Clicquot Grande Dame as a fitting accompaniment; or, if you feel like going a bit wild, a lavish, lively Muscat de Rivesaltes.

3. Gently stir the flour into the mixture. Grease and flour a baking sheet.

4. Place spoonfuls of the mixture onto the baking sheet and use a spatula to spread thin, even circles of dough.

Strawberry Tulips

5. Bake the pastry in a hot oven for 2–3 minutes. Lift each one from the baking sheet and drape over an upturned bowl to cool into the shape of a little basket.

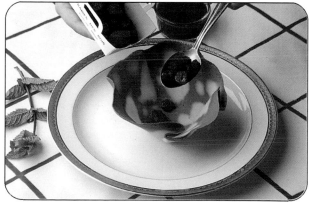

6. Fill the shells with wild strawberries, and garnish with mint leaves. Serve accompanied by raspberry coulis with a tablespoon of honey swirled into it.

Blueberry and

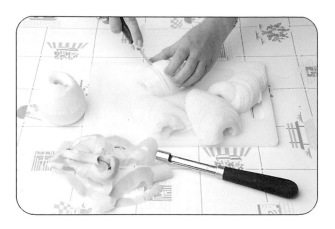

1. Peel, core and very thinly slice the apples.

Ingredients:
4 yellow apples
1½ pints/500 g
   blueberries
6½ tbsp/100 g sugar
¾ cup/200 ml water
8 crêpes
   (see basic recipe)
8¾ oz/250 g pastry
   cream (see basic
   recipe)
3½ tbsp/50 g butter
ground cinnamon
confectioners' sugar
mint

Serves 4
Preparation time: 20 minutes
Cooking time: 10 minutes
Difficulty: ✳ ✳

2. Reserve several whole blueberries to fill the crêpes. Put the rest of the blueberries, the sugar and the water into a blender and purée. Strain this blueberry coulis and set it aside.

Blueberries, with their slightly acidic taste, grow wild in both Europe and the United States. There are also some large-berried cultivated varieties. They are very low in calories, rich in vitamins B and C, and contain a pigment that is good for night vision. These crêpes are not only delicious, but also give you cats' eyes....

Our chef says that when preparing the pastry cream, you should remove the pan from the heat before adding the butter to be sure of achieving a really creamy mixture. A useful little trick: If you are preparing the pastry cream in advance, cover its surface with confectioners' sugar to prevent a skin from forming. Butter the baking sheet lightly so that the crêpes do not stick.

Use a Golden Delicious apple because they are sweet enough to offset the tartness of the blueberries, and they withstand baking well.

This dessert should be served hot, straight out of the oven. Crêpes please everyone—children and grown-ups alike—so give them all a treat with these divinely fruity Blueberry and Apple Crêpes.

It can be difficult to choose the right wine to serve with a dessert. Follow the advice of our wine expert, and offer a little glass of Calvados, which marvelously highlights the flavor of apples.

3. Place 4 crêpes on a lightly buttered baking sheet, and spread 2 tbsp of pastry cream on each.

4. Distribute a spoonful of blueberries on the pastry cream on each crêpe.

Apple Crêpes

5. Cover each with another crêpe, then arrange the apple slices on top in a spiral pattern.

6. Brush the sliced apples with melted butter and sprinkle with just a touch of ground cinnamon. Sprinkle with confectioners' sugar and place in a hot oven for about 15 minutes. Garnish with mint leaves and serve with the blueberry coulis.

Grilled Figs with

Ingredients:
12 fresh plump figs
4 tsp/20 ml kirsch
½ cup plus 2 tbsp/
  150 g sugar
4 egg yolks
6½ tbsp/100 ml
  crème fraîche
3 tbsp ground
  almonds
1 bunch of mint
sugar for sprinkling
  on fig halves

1. Cut the figs in half and place them in a baking dish. Sprinkle with kirsch, then a little sugar, and place in a very hot oven for 3–4 minutes.

Serves 4
Preparation time: 20 minutes
Cooking time: 5 minutes
Difficulty: ✳ ✳

2. In a saucepan, whisk the egg yolks energetically over very low heat.

The fig tree, with its plump tear-drop fruits and large rounded leaves, appears in the Old Testament. It came originally from the East and spread around the Mediterranean Basin. The Romans enjoyed figs with cooked ham or force-fed geese, the Phoenicians munched dried figs during their long sea voyages, and the Corinthians even mixed them—fraudulently—with grapes that they exported to Venice in the 15th century. With this recipe, however, satisfaction is guaranteed and your pleasure will be unadulterated.

Figs are sweet and nourishing, rich in iron and vitamin C, and particularly good for the respiratory tract.

Our chef advises you to bake the figs in a hot oven until they are three-quarters cooked; they should still be firm when removed from the oven. Whisk the sabayon continuously over a low heat. Finally, brown the dish of figs and sabayon briefly under the grill, and serve immediately. This dessert cannot be reheated.

Grilled Figs with Almond Sabayon is a rather unusual dessert, which will enchant your guests with its attractive appearance and warm flavors.

According to our wine expert, try serving a Barsac Château Climens—it will complement the figs beautifully.

3. Add the rest of the sugar to the egg yolks, and continue beating and very gently heating them.

4. Add 2 tbsp/30 ml of the crème fraîche. Again beat very vigorously.

Almond Sabayon

5. While continuing to whisk over a very low heat, sprinkle the ground almonds into the sabayon.

6. Pour the sabayon onto an ovenproof serving dish. Arrange the fig halves on it, then place under the grill for a few minutes. Garnish with mint leaves and serve.

Sautéed Figs with

1. *Lightly and evenly sauté the figs in 1 tbsp of the butter, then set aside.*

Ingredients:
4 plump figs
¾ cup plus 1 tbsp/
   200 g butter
6½ tbsp/100 g sugar
juice of half a lemon
3 tbsp fresh
   pistachios
6½ tbsp/100 ml
   boukha
2 cups/500 ml
   pistachio ice cream

Serves 4
Preparation time: 15 minutes
Cooking time: 10 minutes
Difficulty: ✶

2. *In a saucepan, caramelize the sugar.*

Boukha is a white fig brandy made in Tunisia, and it is highly prized and widely consumed throughout North Africa. Figs are available on the market from the end of June until mid-October. There are several different types but, whichever you buy, remember that a firm stem is an indication of freshness.

Fresh figs are energy-giving, and rich in fruit sugar, iron, magnesium, calcium, potassium, and vitamins A, B, and C. They have tonic properties and are recommended for people taking part in sports. Take care to sauté the figs evenly on all sides. They are very delicate, so to avoid burning them, use very low heat. Or, instead of sautéing the fruits, they could be roasted in a hot oven for ten minutes.

Our chef advises you to make the caramel without water, if possible. Pure sugar will turn golden brown more quickly and have a more intense caramel flavor. Watch the color to determine the right moment to add the butter. If the caramel becomes too dark, it will be bitter and spoil the subtle flavors of the dessert.

Sautéed Figs with Pistachio and Boukha is quick to make, and should be prepared just before serving so that your guests can enjoy the delicious sensation of mingled hot and cold. An elegant and impressive dish, with a subtle combination of flavors, it will be enhanced by a little glass of well-chilled boukha.

3. *When the caramel turns a light brown, stir in the remaining butter, and then add the lemon juice. Stir together vigorously.*

4. *Introduce the pistachios into the caramel sauce and cook over a low heat.*

Pistachio and Boukha

5. Pour in the boukha and remove the caramel sauce from the heat.

6. Just before serving, arrange small scoops of pistachio ice cream in the center of the serving dish, cut open the figs and pour a spoonful of pistachio caramel sauce into each one. Serve.

Two-Toned

1. Allow the vanilla ice cream to soften slightly, then spread all of it onto one of the meringue disks, smoothing it around the sides.

Ingredients:
2 cups/500 ml vanilla ice cream
3 meringue disks, 6-7 in/15-18 cm diameter (see basic recipe for Italian meringue)
2 cups/500 ml black currant sorbet
¾ cup/200 ml heavy cream
6½ tbsp/100 g superfine sugar
red-fruit coulis (see basic recipe)

Serves 8
Preparation time: 20 minutes
Chilling time: 1 hour
Difficulty: ✳ ✳

2. Place the second meringue disk on top of the vanilla ice cream.

This ice cream cake, with its rounded shape and snowy whiteness, is named after the French Vacherin cheese which it resembles, and provides a witty and sophisticated end to your supper.

If you plan to make all the elements of this gâteau from scratch, including the ice cream, sorbet, and meringue, count on spending a whole morning in the kitchen. You must also take into account the fact that the ice cream and sorbet require a minimum of 12 hours' freezing, so you will have to prepare the dessert the day before it is needed. However, even novice cooks can make this great classic, if they buy ready-made ingredients. In any case, your children will enjoy helping you assemble them into a tower of mouthwatering delight, ready for its dreamy coating of crème chantilly.

All that remains is to invite round your best-loved friends to share this luscious Two-Toned Vacherin with you and your family.

Our wine expert suggests uncorking a Champagne Veuve Clicquot Carte d'Or, and let its sparkling bubbles complement this elegant desert.

3. Cover it with the black currant sorbet and again smooth well with a spatula.

4. Cover the black currant sorbet with the third meringue disk.

Vacherin

5. Whisk the cream into a chantilly (see basic recipe) while gradually adding the superfine sugar.

6. Using a pastry bag and nozzle, coat the whole Vacherin with the crème chantilly, garnish, and place in the freezer. Take it out 15 minutes before serving on a bed of red-fruit coulis.

Caribbean

1. For the mousse, combine the egg yolks and sugar in a bowl, and whisk together very vigorously.

Ingredients:
1 sheet coconut
   biscuit (see basic
   recipe)
half a grapefruit
mandarin or
   tangerine jelly
*For the mandarin
   mousse:*
10 egg yolks
1 cup/250 g superfine
   sugar
4 cups/1 liter
   mandarin juice
¾ cup/100 g
   powdered milk
2 tbsp/35 g gelatin
2 cups/500 ml heavy
   cream

Serves 6
Preparation time: 35 minutes
Cooking time: 10 minutes
Chilling time: 3–4 hours
Difficulty: ✳ ✳ ✳

The name of this dreamy gâteau conjures up images of romantic islands suffused with sunny perfumes and flavors.

The mandarin family includes, of course, tangerines. All mandarins are low in calories, rich in vitamin C and calcium, and give off a delicious scent—but any fruit that is sharp in taste and brightly colored can be used here, so there are many possible variations.

Our chef recommends that you continuously whisk the mixture of egg yolks, fruit juice, and sugar while whisking heating it until the simmering point is reached. Be careful that the mixture does not thicken too much, which would mean it would also become too dark in color, spoiling the pale orange effect.

If you like, use a slice of pink grapefruit to garnish the top of the gâteau. There are sure to be cries of admiration when you bring this sunny dessert to the table. It is so light and airy that it melts in the mouth, and your guests will be in a transport of delight.

And what better to accompany the Caribbean Delight than a glass of freshly squeezed grapefruit juice!

2. Pour the mandarin juice into a saucepan, stir in the powdered milk, and heat.

3. When the juice is boiling, pour it onto the egg yolks and sugar while whisking continuously. Blend well, then transfer back into the saucepan.

4. Dissolve the gelatin in cold water. Stir it into the juice and egg yolk mixture and then, whisking continuously, heat the mixture to make a crème anglaise (see basic recipe). Allow to cool.

Delight

5. Cut out a circle of coconut biscuit to fit inside a cake ring and line the sides of the ring (¾ of its height) with a strip of biscuit. Cut a neat slice of grapefruit and place it in the freezer. Whisk the cream into a chantilly (see basic recipe) and fold into the cooled crème anglaise.

6. Fill the cake ring with the mandarin mousse, smooth the top and place the grapefruit slice in the center. Cover with parchment paper to press the grapefruit into the surface of the gâteau. Refrigerate for 3–4 hours, coat with mandarin jelly and serve.

Délices

1. For the cream, combine the eggs and sugar, then add the arrowroot. Split the vanilla bean and infuse it in the milk. Proceed as for a pastry cream (see basic recipe). Set aside to cool. When the cream is tepid, add half the butter, and allow to cool completely.

Ingredients:
4 yellow apples
1 tbsp butter
3 ½ tbsp/50 g sugar
⅓ cup/80 ml Calvados
1 sheet almond biscuit
  (see basic recipe)
¾ cup/200 ml fondant
10½ oz/300 g almond
  paste
red and blue coloring
For the cream filling:
3 eggs
½ cup plus 2 tbsp/
  150 g sugar
2 tbsp/50 g arrowroot
1 vanilla bean
2 cups/500 ml milk
1 cup/250 g butter
½ cup/125 ml heavy cream

Serves 8
Preparation time: 1 hour 30 minutes
Cooking time: 15 minutes
Difficulty: ✷ ✷ ✷

This magnificent gâteau, with its French tricolor decoration, has been created especially for you by our master *pâtissier*. Here are a few hints to help: Sauté the apples until just light golden, then cool them completely before placing them on the cream filling. Also, make sure the pastry cream has cooled completely before adding the second lot of butter to it, then blend the mixture thoroughly. Instead of an almond biscuit, one could substitute a génoise.

Once the gâteau has been assembled, you are ready for the final operation—the decoration. The key here is speed. Prepare miniature pastry bags of parchment paper in advance, and fill them with the red- and blue-colored fondant. The fondant must be neither too hot nor too cold but, as our chef says, at "the temperature of your tongue." The white fondant must still warm when it is ladled and smoothed over the gâteau. Immediately after adding the red and blue decoration, draw the point of a knife through the fondant to create a pattern.

Your artistic touch will earn you well-deserved compliments when you bring this impressive French Delight to the table. Such a beautiful dessert obviously calls for a great champagne: A Veuve Clicquot Grande Dame.

2. Peel and quarter the apples and sauté in the butter and sugar. Flambé the pan with the Calvados, allow to cool, and refrigerate. To complete the filling, add the rest of the butter to the cream mixture; whisk for 8-10 minutes into a thoroughly blended paste. Whisk the heavy cream into a chantilly and fold it into the filling.

3. Cut out 2 pieces of almond biscuit to fit the cake form. Place 1 layer in the form and cover with some of the cream filling, spreading it up the sides of the form.

4. Arrange the apple quarters on the filling, and cover them with the rest of the cream. Top with the second piece of almond biscuit and refrigerate.

de France

5. Roll out the almond paste and cover the gâteau with it. Heat the fondant over a double boiler. Add red coloring to a spoonful of fondant and blue to another.

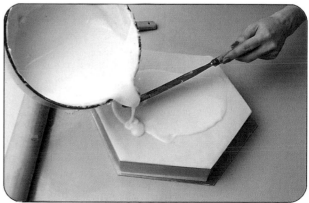

6. Fill 2 parchment paper cones with the 2 colored fondants. Remove the gâteau from its mold, quickly pour the warm white fondant over it, and smooth the surface with a spatula. Working quickly, make parallel red and blue lines on the gâteau, and draw the point of a knife across them.

Raspberry and

1. For the ganache, heat the cream and add the white chocolate, stirring continuously until the chocolate melts and the mixture has cooled. Beat in the butter in small pieces with an electric whisk. Add the egg yolks and blend well.

2. Prepare an Italian meringue according to the basic recipe and use a wooden spoon to gently fold it into the ganache. Bake a chocolate génoise, again according to the basic recipe.

Ingredients:
1 chocolate génoise
To soak: 1½ tbsp/10 g bitter cocoa; 6½ tbsp/ 100 ml light corn syrup
To garnish: 3½ oz/100 g green almond paste; whole raspberries
White ganache filling:
8¾ oz/250 g light cream
1 generous lb/500 g white chocolate
1 cup/250 g butter
2 egg yolks
8¾ oz/250 g Italian meringue
Raspberry filling:
⅓ cup/125 g raspberry jelly
3½ tbsp/50 ml raspberry brandy
4 leaves gelatin
7 oz/200 g frozen raspberries

Serves 8
Preparation time: 40 minutes
Cooking time: 5 minutes
Chilling time: 1 hour
Difficulty: ✳ ✳ ✳

A scarlet coronet of raspberries adds a touch of gaiety to this mouthwatering gâteau, which can be served at the end of any kind of meal, from informal to sophisticated.

Our chef recommends using frozen raspberries for the fruit filling because he finds they are easier to chop. The whole berries for the garnish should, of course, be fresh.

The raspberry jelly must be dissolved: For every ¼ cup/100 g of jelly, add 6½ tbsp/100 g water and two leaves of gelatin. This will produce a jellied mixture sufficiently transparent for the raspberries to show through.

Take the chef's advice and serve this luscious dessert with a raspberry coulis (see basic recipe). The contrast between the acidity of the fruit and the sweetness of the gâteau offset each other perfectly.

Our wine expert recommends drinking a Champagne Veuve Clicquot Carte Jaune with this spectacular Raspberry and Chocolate Gâteau.

3. Cut the génoise horizontally in half. Place 1 layer in the bottom of a cake ring (the other can be used in another recipe). Stir the cocoa into the corn syrup and lightly moisten the génoise with it.

4. Cover the moistened génoise and the sides of the cake ring with the ganache filling, and set aside.

Chocolate Gâteau

5. Dissolve the gelatin in ½ cup/125 ml water. Combine the raspberry jelly, brandy, and dissolved gelatin. Chop the frozen raspberries and pour ¾ of the jelly over them. Stir briskly.

6. Quickly pour the raspberry mixture into the mold, smooth with a spatula, and top with the rest of the jelly. Refrigerate until firm, then remove the cake ring and cover the sides of the gâteau with green almond paste. Garnish with a few whole raspberries.

Dijon

1. In a small saucepan, heat the black currant purée and the crème fraîche.

2. Soften the gelatin leaves in cold water, then add to the black currant mixture. When the gelatin has dissolved, remove the pan from the heat and allow the mixture to cool.

3. Separate the eggs and reserve the whites. Add the sugar to the yolks and whisk into a sabayon (see glossary) over very low heat.

Ingredients:
1 almond biscuit
 (see basic recipe)
For the filling:
1 cup plus 2 tbsp/
 250 g black currant
 purée
2 tbsp/25 ml crème
 fraîche
5 leaves gelatin
5 eggs
3½ tbsp/50 g
 superfine sugar
Italian meringue
 (see basic recipe)
1¼ cups/300 ml
 cream
To garnish:
black currant jelly
whole currants

Serves 6
Preparation time: 25 minutes
Cooking time: 5 minutes
Chilling time: 4–5 hours
Difficulty: ✶ ✶ ✶

This dessert is worthy of its name: It really is supreme! All that is needed to prepare this magnificent, glistening creation is a little care and attention.

When you add the black currant purée mixture to the sabayon, continue stirring with a wooden spoon in a figure-eight movement for three to four minutes over low heat.

To prevent the almond biscuit from sticking to the cake ring, line it ahead of time with parchment paper.

Place the mousse filling in the refrigerator for at least 20 minutes, or until it is cold to the touch, before turning it into the cake ring. From time to time take it out of the refrigerator and stir it with a whisk.

As long as you follow all these pieces of advice, you will have no problems in producing a marvelous Dijon Supreme that tastes as good as it looks.

Follow our wine expert's advice, too, and uncork a bottle of Champagne Veuve Clicquot Carte Jaune.

4. Pour the black currant mixture into the sabayon and stir until well-combined.

Supreme

5. Use the egg whites to prepare an Italian meringue; whisk the heavy cream into a chantilly (see basic recipes for both). Fold the meringue and the crème chantilly into the cold black currant sabayon with a wooden spatula.

6. Line the bottom and sides of a cake ring with almond biscuit, and fill with the mixture. Refrigerate 4–5 hours to set, then top with a layer of black currant jelly. Garnish and serve well-chilled.

Jockey

1. *Divide the puff pastry into 2 pieces. Roll out 1 of the pieces and line a tart form with it. Prick the pastry with a fork and bake in the oven. Roll out the second piece of pastry and cut into a lattice.*

Ingredients:
14 oz/400 g puff pastry
  (see basic recipe)
beaten egg for glaze
2 cups/500 ml pastry
  cream (see basic
  recipe)
1 cup plus 6 tbsp/330 ml
  crème chantilly
  (see basic recipe)
an assortment of fruit in
  season: strawberries,
  raspberries, bananas,
  mangoes, red currants,
  oranges, kiwis
1¾ oz/50 g clear glaze

Serves 6
Preparation time: 20 minutes
Cooking time: 25 minutes
Difficulty: ✳ ✳

2. *Cut a round out of the lattice, the same size as the tart form, and brush lightly with beaten egg. Bake on a baking sheet in a moderate oven.*

This fruit salad of stunning colors and heady scents, piled onto a puff pastry tart deliciously filled with pastry cream, will make a triumphant end to any dinner party.

The addition of crème chantilly to the pastry cream makes it thinner and lighter—you will be surprised by the difference it makes.

Toss the banana slices in lemon juice to prevent them from becoming discolored. Moreover, the acidity of the lemon will intensify and improve the flavor of the fruit.

If you do not have a lattice-work pastry-cutter, cut out thin strips of pastry and arrange them in a lattice pattern by hand. Your children may even be delighted to give you a hand. One important piece of advice from the chef: Be sure to bake this latticed "lid" in a moderate oven.

Have fun arranging the fruits in patterns that look like the racing colors on jockeys' caps. In place of cake glaze, you may choose to glaze the tart with apricot jelly. You can confidently place your bet on this easily-made dessert—it's a certain winner!

To celebrate a victory in the traditional manner, champagne is called for, so take our wine expert's advice and serve a Veuve Clicquot rosé.

3. *Prepare the pastry cream and crème chantilly according to the basic recipes. Whisk the pastry cream vigorously; with a spatula, gently fold in the chantilly.*

4. *Fill the tart case with this mixture.*

Tart

5. Clean, peel and slice the fruit as necessary, and place it attractively on top of the filling.

6. Melt the glaze and brush the fruit with it to give the tart a glistening appearance. Place the latticed round of pastry at an angle on the tart, so that it looks like a half-opened basket.

Smuggler's

1. Bake a chocolate génoise according to the basic recipe in sheet form. For the mousse, combine the egg yolks, chestnut cream and chestnut paste in a bowl and whisk very vigorously.

Ingredients:
1 chocolate génoise
   (see basic recipe)
syrup to moisten
8 glazed chestnuts
3½ oz/100 g semi-sweet
   baking chocolate
1¾ oz/50 g sweet baking
   chocolate
For the mousse filling:
4 egg yolks
8¾ oz/250 g chestnut-
   flavored pastry cream
   (see basic recipe)
8¾ oz/250 g chestnut
   paste
1 cup/250 g butter
8¾ oz/250 g Italian
   meringue
   (see basic recipe)

Serves 6
Preparation time: 40 minutes
Chilling time: 1 hour
Difficulty: ✳ ✳ ✳

Although the name of this dessert suggests mystery and stealth, hidden coves, secret passages, and nocturnal adventures across densely wooded frontiers, preparing this wonderful chocolate gâteau involves no undercover activities. In fact, the chef wants to reassure you straight away: The boat-like shape of the gâteau is just a whim of his, and you should feel free to use any cake form you fancy.

He does stress that it is essential to melt the chocolate in a bain-marie over very low heat. You can draw a pattern over the surface of the gâteau with the point of a knife before the chocolate hardens, as shown in the picture here—but use a very light touch.

Whatever shape you choose for your Smuggler's Barque, your guests are sure to be captivated by its dark beauty. To set off the chocolate and chestnuts, our wine expert suggests a Monbazillac.

2. Add the softened butter and whisk steadily until the mixture is thoroughly blended.

3. With a wooden spatula, fold the Italian meringue into the chesnut mixture.

4. Line the bottom of a form with the génoise, moisten with a little syrup, and half-fill with the chestnut mousse. Arrange 5 of the glazed chestnuts on the mousse and top with the remaining filling. Cover with a layer of génoise and refrigerate 1 hour.

Barque

5. Melt the chocolates in separate bowls over hot water. Make a small cone of parchment paper and fill it with the milk chocolate.

6. Turn out the gâteau. Coat it quickly with the darker chocolate, then draw a pattern over the surface with milk chocolate. Garnish with 3 whole glazed chestnuts.

Chocolate

1. Soften the butter and grate the zest of both lemons into it.

Ingredients:
7½ tbsp/110 g butter
2 lemons
½ cup plus 1 tsp/
  80 g confectioners'
  sugar
2 egg yolks
1 cup minus 1 tbsp/
  160 g ground
  almonds
1¼ cups plus 2 tbsp/
  170 g flour
For the ganache:
1 cup/250 ml heavy
  cream
1 generous lb/500 g
  semi-sweet baking
  chocolate

Serves 6
Preparation time: 15 minutes
Cooking time: 15 minutes
Difficulty: ✶ ✶

2. Add the confectioners' sugar, and blend thoroughly.

The original Linzertorte is an Austrian confection with a rich, crumbly base including ground nuts, raspberry jam filling, and lattice decoration.

A French touch is added to this version in the form of a ganache, which beautifully complements the rather short pastry. The most difficult part of preparing any kind of *pâtisserie*, in this case meaning sweet baked goods, is achieving a mixture of the right consistency. The dough for this recipe must be soft and smooth.

If you prefer keeping to tradition, line a tart form with the pastry, fill it with raspberry preserves, and decorate the top with a lattice formed by squeezing the dough through a pastry bag. When baked, the lattice takes on an attractive wavy pattern. Sprinkle it with confectioners' sugar as soon as you have taken it out of the oven.

Those who prefer a change from tradition can experiment with different types of ganache, using milk chocolate, white chocolate, praline, and so forth.

Enjoying such a mouthwatering treat is only slightly sinful! So go on, spoil yourself and your family, just this once….

A cup of good, hot coffee goes well with these chocolaty tarts.

3. Add the egg yolks and stir the mixture vigorously.

4. Pour the ground almonds into the mixture while continuing to beat with a wooden spoon. Add the flour and beat again; allow to rest for about 1 hour.

Linzers

5. Fill small pastry forms with the mixture and bake in a moderate oven for 20 minutes.

6. Melt the chocolate over hot water and pour onto the heavy cream. Combine thoroughly and allow to rest. Once the ganache has cooled, decorate the top of the Linzers with a pastry bag and nozzle.

Coconut

1. Combine the ground almonds and 6½ tbsp/100 g sugar in a bowl.

Ingredients:
8½ tbsp/100 g ground
   almonds
½ cup/120 g sugar
6½ tbsp/100 g butter,
   softened
1 egg
1 tbsp flour
2 tbsp/30 ml white
   rum
1 cup plus 2 tbsp/
   100 g grated
   coconut
2 egg yolks

Serves 6
Preparation time: 30 minutes
Cooking time: 20 minutes
Difficulty: ✳ ✳

2. Add the softened butter and blend the mixture thoroughly with a wooden spoon.

In French, these little cakes are called rockers, or little rocks, because of their appearance, not their texture! They are also known as *congeals*—and the same dough can be used as a topping for tarts.

If possible, use fresh coconut because of its immeasurably superior taste. The butter should be just the right consistency, neither too hard nor too soft, but creamy and still slightly firm. Leave it at room temperature for a few hours, then beat it to make it easier to work with.

This recipe is child's play—the only utensil you need is a wooden spoon. If you like, you can form the dough into little *galettes*, or flat shingles, stick them together with ganache, and give them a chocolate coating.

Another suggestion from the chef is for a coconut and banana tart: Line a tart form with the coconut dough from this recipe, fill with banana slices tossed in lemon juice, then cover with more dough. The result is delicious! This is a versatile recipe that offers a wide range of mouthwatering possibilities.

This is yet another occasion for opening a Champagne Veuve Clicquot!

3. Beat in the whole egg.

4. Gradually add the flour, stirring continuously. Pour in the white rum.

"Rochers"

5. Add ¾ of the grated coconut, the remaining 1½ tbsp/20 g sugar, and 2 the egg yolks. Beat the dough energetically.

6. Use your hands to form the dough into small balls, and roll them in the rest of the grated coconut. Arrange on a baking sheet covered with parchment paper and bake for 20 minutes in a moderate oven.

Minted Fruit

1. Set aside the grapes. Peel the other fruit as necessary. Chop the larger fruit into small pieces.

Ingredients:
1 bunch black grapes
1 bunch white grapes
1 pineapple
2 peaches
2 nectarines
7 oz/200 g
   raspberries
7 oz/200 g
   strawberries
6½ tbsp/100 g sugar
1 bunch mint

Serves 4
Preparation time: 15 minutes
Chilling time: 1 hour
Difficulty: ✶

2. Liquefy half of the fruits in an electric blender and add the sugar.

Soup must be hot, you think. But mint sounds cool and fresh. In fact, this is not a hot soup for the start of a meal, but a divinely fruity concoction to end it on a note of sheer beauty. The unexpected taste of the chopped mint makes this a delightfully different kind of coulis.

Our chef points out that the fruit must remain really firm; thus the dessert must be made shortly before serving. If the fruit is allowed to wait too long, it will lose its optimum flavor and appearance.

As a final touch, squeeze a little lemon juice over the fruit and coulis at the last moment. The slight acidity will provide a welcome sharp taste after a rather rich meal.

Of course, you can use any kinds of fruit you like. Enjoy yourself choosing a combination of tastes and colors to suit the occasion. Moreover, Minted Fruit Gazpacho is low in calories, so you can enjoy it without feeling guilty

Our wine expert thinks that an extra-brut champagne will go perfectly with this combination of fruit and mint.

3. Remove the mint leaves from the stalks and chop the leaves finely. Add to the fruit coulis in the blender and briefly whirl.

4. Press the fruit coulis through a fine sieve to remove any seeds and set aside.

Gazpacho

5. Remove the grapes from the stalks and wash the fruit thoroughly.

6. Add the grapes and the rest of the peeled and chopped fruit to minted fruit coulis, chill in the refrigerator, and serve very cold.

Orange Omelet Soufflé

1. Remove the zest from the orange and julienne it. Blanch in 2 or 3 successive changes of water, then cook with the grenadine syrup until the peel is soft and the syrup reduced. Drain and reserve.

Ingredients:
1 orange
6½ tbsp/100 ml grenadine syrup
chocolate sauce (see basic recipe)
For the soufflé:
6 eggs
6½ tbsp/100 g sugar
6½ tbsp/100 ml Grand Marnier
7 oz/200 ml chocolate ice cream

Serves 6
Preparation time: 25 minutes
Cooking time: 15 minutes
Chilling time: 2 hours
Difficulty: ✷ ✷

For those who still believe that making a soufflé requires great skill, here is a recipe to prove the opposite. It is so simple that you will wish you had tried it before.

Just to reassure you, our chef has shared a few secrets: Prepare the chocolate ice cream roll well in advance and leave it in the freezer for as long as possible. It must be very hard in order not to melt too quickly when the dessert is baked in the oven.

Add the sugar to the egg whites only after they have started to become firm; then whisk vigorously until stiff. The success of the dessert depends on the strength of your wrist, so to speak. To ensure that the yolks are equally firm, heat them very gently while beating them with sugar.

Combine the beaten egg yolks and egg whites with the most delicate touch possible for a mixture that is light and airy.

Blanch the orange zest in a little sugared water to remove some of its bitterness. After bringing to a boil, repeat the operation in sugared water. The Grenadine syrup is optional, but it adds a beautiful color. Cook the zest very slowly.

The Orange Omelet Soufflé with Chocolate Ice Cream is such an impressive way to end a meal! Your friends will hardly be able to stop talking about the combination of orange and chocolate—another reason for serving a special treat: A Banyuls Grand Cru!

2. Separate the eggs. Add half of the sugar to the yolks and whisk over very gentle heat (bain-marie) until the mixture falls from the spoon in a ribbon.

3. Add the Grand Marnier to the yolks and stir the mixture vigorously.

4. Whisk the egg whites into soft peaks, gradually adding the rest of the sugar.

with Chocolate Ice Cream

5. Form the chocolate ice cream into a long roll and secure in freezer wrap. Place in the freezer to become very hard. Gently fold the egg whites into the yolk mixture with a wooden spoon to complete the soufflé.

6. Pour a layer of the soufflé mixture onto an ovenproof serving dish. Place the unwrapped roll of chocolate ice cream in the center and cover with a thick layer of soufflé mixture. Bake in a moderately hot oven for 15 minutes, top with the orange syrup and serve very hot accompanied by a chocolate sauce.

Apple

1. Peel, core and quarter the apples. Cook ¾ of them in a saucepan containing the sugar, a little water, and a little butter. Dice the rest of the apples and brown in butter in another saucepan. Soften the raisins in a little warm water or Calvados.

Ingredients:
8 apples
1 tbsp sugar
butter for sautéing
½ cup plus 1 tbsp/
   100 g raisins
6½ tbsp/100 g butter
1 loaf of stale bread,
   sliced
½ tsp ground
   cinnamon
1 lemon
1 egg
1 cup/250 ml crème
   anglaise
   (see basic recipe)

Serves 6
Preparation time: 35 minutes
Cooking time: 40 minutes
Chilling time: 2 hours
Difficulty: ✲ ✲

Charlottes derive from a late-18th century English dessert which was possibly named in honor of the wife of King George III. And this fine old recipe was developed by the great chef Escoffier. It is somewhat unusual in that the ladyfingers that traditionally line the mold, or individual forms in this case, have been replaced by bread.

The water added to the butter and sugar in which you cook the apple quarters will prevent them from sticking to the bottom of the pan. Taste the apples and their sauce: If they seem too sour, add a little more sugar. If you like, you can soak the raisins in Calvados instead of water. This will give your Charlotte an extra fragrance. Do not forget to blanch the lemon zest to remove its bitterness.

Be sure to soak the bread slices thoroughly with melted butter before putting them under the grill so that they stay soft. Wait until the apple and raisin mixture has cooled before adding the egg, which helps bind the filling and makes the Apple Charlotte easier to turn out of its molds.

Charlottes are to be found on the best menus everywhere today. This home-made version, thanks to Escoffier, will be one of the tastiest of all!

Serve your guests a small glass of Calvados Père Magloire with this apple dessert.

2. Melt the butter and brush the slices of bread generously with it; then toast the bread under the grill.

3. Add the raisins to the diced apple and sprinkle with ground cinnamon.

4. Cut the bread slices into triangles and line the bottom of a individual forms with them. Shave the zest from the lemon and cut into fine slices. Blanch in 2 or 3 successive changes of water, and drain.

Charlotte

5. Press the cooked apple quarters through a sieve. Add the diced apple, raisins, and lemon zest to the apple pulp, then incorporate the egg and mix well.

6. Fill the forms with this mixture and bake for about 20 minutes in a moderate oven. Allow to cool, then refrigerate. Serve cold, accompanied by a crème anglaise and caramelized apple quarters.

Apple

1. Sift the flour into a bowl. Add 2 egg yolks, the yeast, butter and a pinch of salt, and mix together. Gradually pour in the beer, stirring continuously. Set in a warm place to rise.

Ingredients:
1½ cups plus 2 tbsp/
   200 g flour
2 egg yolks
1 tsp yeast
2 tbsp butter,
   softened
1 glass beer
6 apples
6½ tbsp/100 g sugar
3½ tbsp/50 ml
   Calvados Père
   Magloire
3 egg whites
salt
oil for deep-frying
sugar for sprinkling
   on fritters

Serves 4
Preparation time: 15 minutes
Cooking time: 20 minutes
Difficulty: ✳ ✳

2. Peel and core the apples and cut them into donut-shaped rings.

This is a special treat for children's birthdays and parties. Pile a big dish high with these golden fritters—children simply can't get enough of them! If you feel like breaking with tradition, you could substitute apples with other fruit, such as pears or bananas, but avoid a juicy fruit, which would make the batter too liquid.

Marinate the apples well in the sweetened Calvados so that they have time to soak up the flavor of the alcohol.

Beer is a leavening agent, so the batter requires only a little yeast, and yet will be beautifully light. The amount of beer needed depends on the consistency of your batter, which must not be too liquid because it has to cover the apple rounds completely. On the other hand, the fritters should be perfectly light.

This is a simple, trouble-free recipe, so you will be able to make Apple Fritters time and time again. Our wine expert recommends serving either Calvados or fruit juice with the fritters—it all depends on the age of your guests.

3. Sprinkle the apple slices with the sugar and then with Calvados, and leave to marinate.

4. Whisk the egg whites into soft peaks, and fold them gently into the beer batter.

Fritters

5. Dip the apple slices in the batter, making sure they are evenly coated, then fry them in hot oil.

6. Sprinkle superfine sugar over the fritters and serve with a raspberry coulis (see basic recipe).

Orange Peel

Ingredients:
3 large oranges
1½ cups/350 g
   superfine sugar
juice of half a lemon
1 tbsp orange-flower
   water
10½ oz/300 g sablée
   pastry (see basic
   recipe)
6 eggs
4 tbsp heavy cream

Serves 8
Preparation time: 20 minutes
Cooking time: 45 minutes
Difficulty: ✶

1. Wash the oranges carefully, then peel them roughly, taking whole rind. Grind the rind in a food processor.

Orange Peel Tart is a lovely round sun to brighten your kitchen and make your guests smile. It has a comforting air about it, and our chef tells us that its "home-made" character is what makes it so special. She grew up in Tunisia and enjoys recreating the delicious cuisine of her childhood.

Like most citrus fruit, oranges can be sweet or sour. Choose whichever kind of oranges you like best, but make sure they are firm, with skins that are quite smooth and shiny and untreated by chemicals. Avoid at all costs oranges that are soft and dull-looking. Don't worry about the bitterness of the orange zest: The resulting marmalade will be sweetened by the sugar and the orange-flower water.

The brightness and straightforward simplicity of this appealing tart will chase away all the grayness of winter days, and its delicious fragrance will envelop any kind of get-together in happiness.

Here is an ideal occasion for proving to your guests that nothing goes better with dessert than a liqueur or a fruit brandy.

2. In a saucepan, combine the ground rind with 1¼ cups/300 g of the sugar, the lemon juice, a glass of water, and the orange-flower water. Bring to a boil and simmer for 30 minutes over very low heat, then remove from the heat and allow to cool.

3. Line a shallow tart pan with the sablée pastry, then prick the bottom with a fork. Set aside.

4. Add the eggs and the rest of the sugar to the rind and stir the mixture vigorously.

Tart

5. Pour in the crème fraîche and again whisk the mixture energetically.

6. Fill the pastry shell with the orange mixture and bake in a moderate oven for about 30 minutes. Serve warm or cold, as desired.

Pear and

1. Carefully peel and core the pears. Rub them with a cut lemon to prevent discoloration. Poach them in a saucepan containing water and ¾ cup plus 1 tbsp/200 g superfine sugar over low heat.

Ingredients:
7 pears
1 lemon
1¼ cups/300 g superfine sugar
3 eggs
1⅓ cups/200 g confectioners' sugar
1 cup plus 2 tbsp/ 200 g ground almonds
6½ tbsp/100 ml heavy cream
7 ladyfingers
1¾ cups/50 g blanched pistachios, unshelled

Serves 7
Preparation time: 20 minutes
Cooking time: 35 minutes
Difficulty: ✶

The pale, melt-in-your-mouth flesh of cooked pears is delicately perfumed and delicious. The first pears appear on the market from mid-July, but their main season is between September and January. In France, pears are the third most popular fruit, in terms of quantity consumed. They are a good source of vitamins B and C and also of potassium. William pears, not too ripe, are ideal for this recipe. You can substitute apples for pears, if you like. Granny Smiths are ideal, because they stay firm when cooked.

The chef's advice on poaching the pears is to plunge them into boiling water and poach for 15 minutes—less if the pears are very ripe. Above all, do not moisten the ladyfingers before placing them in the poached pears, or they will be too soft and disintegrate.

The Pear and Pistachio Casserole is a simple, informal dish that is easy to make and very nourishing. It makes a pleasant end to a light meal.

Our wine expert suggests serving an iced pear brandy.

2. Separate the eggs, reserving the whites. Add the confectioner's sugar to the yolks and stir vigorously.

3. Add the ground almonds and heavy cream to the yolk mixture. Stir vigorously again.

4. Whisk the egg whites together with rest of the sugar, and fold them gently into the egg yolk mixture using a wooden spatula.

Pistachio Casserole

5. When the pears have cooked and drained, insert a ladyfinger into the middle of each, and arrange the pears in a buttered gratin dish.

6. Cover the pears with the prepared mixture. Cook in a slow oven for about 25 minutes. Shell and chop the pistachios and sprinkle over the pear gratin after baking. Serve warm.

Pâte à Tuiles

Ingredients:
scant ½ cup/75 g
    confectioners' sugar
2 tbsp/30 g butter
2 egg whites
⅓ cup/40 g flour, sifted
vanilla extract

Preparation time: 10 minutes
Cooking time: 10 minutes
Difficulty: ✴✴✴

1. Vigorously whisk the confectioners' sugar and softened butter together. Add the egg whites and continue to beat; the mixture should be homogeneous, creamy, and smooth. Mix in the flour, then the salt and a few drops of vanilla extract.

2. Lightly grease and flour the baking sheet. Place spoonfuls of the mixture on the tray and use a spatula to spread it into thin, even circles.

Ideal for beautiful presentations of fruit, ice cream, or other light treats, *pâté a tuiles*, literally "tile batter," needs to be prepared with care.

The butter should be cold when you prepare the dough so it does not become too liquid. Refrigerate the batter for 30 minutes before spreading it on the cookie sheets and baking. This is not absolutely necessary, but it is one more way of assuring the success of these not-so-simple pastry forms.

The baking sheet should be greased and floured. Place a spoonful of the pastry mixture on the tray and use a straight spatula to flatten it well, making sure that every portion is the same thickness.

After baking, the pastry "tiles" quickly cool and become stiff, so do not delay. Removing them from the tray is a delicate operation. Using one or two spatulas, quickly lift the circles and drape them over an upturned bowl, in a bowl, or over a rolling pin to give them the shape you require. Do not hesitate to use your hands to form them.

3. Bake for about 10 minutes in a hot oven. Remove the pastry rounds while they are hot using a spatula and place them in or on a form so that they take on the desired shape: tulips, bowls etc.

Raspberry Coulis

Ingredients:
1 generous lb/500 g
  raspberries
¾ cup/200 ml water
3½ tbsp/50 ml raspberry
  brandy
3½ tbsp/50 g superfine
  sugar

1. Wash the raspberries carefully; drain well. Put them in a food processor, add the water, and blend.

Preparation time: 5 minutes
Chilling time: 20 minutes
Difficulty: ✳

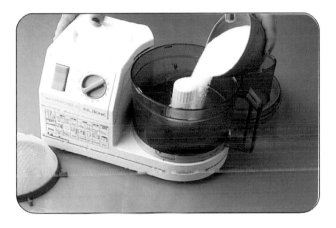

2. Pour in the brandy and sugar and blend a few moments more until the fruit is thoroughly puréed.

The word "coulis" was at one time used as a general term for all sauces. Some cooks maintain that it originally referred to the juices produced when meat is cooked. Others think it referred to a thin purée made of fish, seafood or meat—and indeed, a coulis can certainly take the form of a soup, if it is made out of a vegetable.

As for raspberry coulis, its delicious perfume enhances a number of desserts, ices, soufflés, gâteaux and other sweet dishes. Furthermore, it is in and of itself delicious, refreshing and full of vitamins.

With its sharp, strong flavor, raspberry coulis also makes an excellent base for a sorbet.

Use this recipe as a starting point for experimentation with other fruits, such as peach, apricot, black currant or kiwi fruit. As long as you choose fully ripe fruit of high quality, the coulis cannot be anything but successful.

3. Pass the coulis through a fine sieve to remove the raspberry seeds. Chill in the refrigerator before serving.

Coconut Biscuit

Ingredients:
3 egg yolks
3 whole eggs
1 generous cup/250 g
  sugar
1⅓ cups/125 g freeze-dried
  shredded coconut
¾ cup+1 tbsp/150 g ground
  almonds
6½ tbsp/50 g flour
7 egg whites
6½ tbsp/100 g butter
For the topping:
grated coconut
confectioners' sugar

Preparation time: 10 minutes
Cooking time: 20 minutes
Difficulty: ✶✶

1. Combine the egg yolks and whole eggs in a large bowl. Pour in the sugar and whisk vigorously to the ribbon stage. Add the shredded coconut.

2. Stir in the ground almonds, then add the flour gradually. Whisk the egg whites into soft peaks, then gently fold them into the mixture with a spatula.

The French word *biscuit* is derived from *bis cuit,* literally indicating that it was originally something twice-cooked. This gave it a hard texture and let it keep longer without spoiling. For centuries, the durable staple eaten by French soldiers and sailors was simply biscuit—exactly what the Roman legionaries knew as "Parthians bread." In the reign of Louis XIV, soldiers were rationed their *biscuit de troupe* or *pain de pierre*, "stone bread."

There is a French expression, *ne pas s'embarquer sans biscuit* ("don't embark without your biscuit"), which recalls the days when sailors had to take large quantities of provisions on board before setting off on a long voyage.

These days, a French *biscuit* is a sponge cake, hardly ever baked twice, and pleasurably soft to bite into.

The chefs offer a few suggestions: The egg whites must be whisked into firm peaks and then immediately folded into the mixture; and the sponge cake must be baked in a moderate oven to ensure that it turns out soft and pliable. This coconut biscuit can be used as part of a more complex gâteau, or just topped with jam and served as is.

3. Generously butter and flour a baking sheet. Pour the biscuit mixture onto it, sprinkle with grated coconut and a little confectioners' sugar, and bake in a moderate oven for about 20 minutes.

Crème Anglaise

Ingredients:
10 egg yolks
vanilla extract
1¼ cups/300 g superfine
   sugar
4 cups/1 liter milk

Preparation time: 5 minutes
Cooking time: 5 minutes
Difficulty: ✳✳

1. Place the yolks in a bowl, add a few drops of vanilla extract, and stir. Add the sugar and whisk vigorously until the sugar dissolves and the mixture becomes pale.

2. Bring the milk to a boil, then pour it into the egg yolks and sugar mixture while whisking vigorously.

Crème anglaise is a custard sauce made of eggs, milk and sugar. It can be enhanced by the addition of many flavors to accompany a wide range of dishes, hot or cold.

Here are a few tips from our chefs to ensure a perfect sauce: Beat the egg yolks and sugar together until they are foamy and pale. Add the milk while it is boiling hot, but slowly so that the eggs do not coagulate, and stir briskly the entire time. When half the milk has been incorporated, the rest can be added more quickly.

Place the saucepan over a very low heat. It is essential to stir continuously, using a wooden spoon, while the custard thickens. The crème anglaise is ready when it coats the spoon.

Do not let the custard boil, as this would cause the egg yolks to separate from the milk. Transfer the sauce immediately into a cold receptacle.

Versatile crème anglaise can accompany brioches or génoise, or be spooned over fruit, puddings, or simple gâteaux, just to name a few ideas.

3. Transfer the mixture to a large saucepan and place over very low heat. Stir continuously with a wooden spoon; do not let the crème anglaise boil. As soon as it starts to thicken, remove from heat. Pour into a cool bowl to keep it from cooking any further.

Crème Chantilly

Ingredients:
2 cups/500 ml cream
3½ tbsp/35 g confectioner's
    sugar
vanilla extract

1. Pour the cold cream into a cold bowl. Sift in the confectioner's sugar.

Preparation time: 5 minutes
Difficulty: ✳

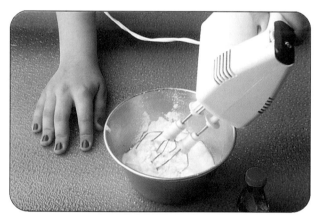

2. Begin beating it with an electric mixer.

Crème chantilly is a classic element for decorating appetizers, entrées, and desserts. The underlying principle could not be simpler: Whip the cream with the sugar very thoroughly. Still, here are a few suggestions to make the process easier:

The cream and the mixing bowl, even the whisk or beaters, should be very cold. Once whipped, store in the refrigerator.

Start whipping slowly and regularly to make the cream double in volume. Increase the speed on the beater until the cream has the consistency of beaten egg whites.

Stop beating at this point so the cream does not turn into butter! Place the crème chantilly in the refrigerator until it is needed. If the whipped cream has liquified slightly, simply beat it again for a few seconds before serving.

3. Once the cream is fairly firm, add a few drops of vanilla extract. Refrigerate until needed.

Italian Meringue

Ingredients:
8 egg whites
2 generous cups/500 g
  sugar
1 vanilla bean
1 glass water

1. Pour the sugar into a saucepan. Add the vanilla bean and glass of water and stir over low heat. When the syrup begins to thicken, scrape down the sugar granules forming on the sides of the pan with a pastry brush dipped in water.

Preparation time: 15 minutes
Cooking time: 10 minutes
Difficulty: ✶✶

When preparing Italian meringue, a candy thermometer is useful. The initial operation consists in heating the sugar to 240 °F/115 °C, or the "soft ball" stage, to form a syrup of the right consistency. If a thermometer is not available, you can check whether the syrup is ready by taking a small spoonful and dropping it in a glass of cold water. If the syrup does not fall apart, but is cohesive enough for you to form a very soft ball with it when you take it out of the water, the syrup is at the soft ball stage.

The second step is to trickle the sugar syrup onto the whisked egg whites while continuing to whisk vigorously until the meringue has completely cooled.

There is nothing particularly difficult about making this smooth, delicious Italian meringue, but you must be energetic and persistent when beating the mixture and continue the entire time it is cooling.

Italian meringue is very versatile: It can be used as a topping for pies, pastries, ice cream or other desserts, or baked as cookies or even bases for use in gâteaux.

2. Watch the syrup carefully as it reaches the "soft ball" stage, or 240 °F/115 °C. Drop a little syrup into a bowl of iced water. It should form a ball that is soft, and not at all brittle.

3. Whisk the egg whites into stiff peaks just as the syrup reaches the soft ball stage. Remove the vanilla bean and trickle the sugar syrup onto the meringue, whisking continuously and very vigorously. Continue beating with an electric mixer until completely cooled.

1. Break the eggs into a bowl. Sprinkle in the sugar while beating with an electric mixer over very low heat until the mixture becomes quite pale.

Ingredients:
4 eggs
½ cup/125 g
    superfine sugar
¾ cup plus 1
    tbsp/100 g flour
7½ tbsp/50 g cocoa
3½ tbsp/50 g butter,
    melted

Preparation time: 30 minutes
Cooking time: 20 minutes
Difficulty: ✷✷

2. Remove from heat, and continue whisking until the mixture is lukewarm. Sift the flour into the mixture, while continuing to stir more gently, by hand.

Génoise is an extremely versatile cake used as a base for many gâteaux and pâtisseries. Start by thoroughly whisking the eggs and sugar over very low heat, either in a warm bowl or over a double boiler. The mixture should become only slightly warm; do not overheat it. Remove from the heat to finish whisking to the ribbon stage.

When the mixture has cooled a little, add the flour very delicately. Stop stirring as soon as the flour is thoroughly incorporated so that the batter keeps its smooth consistency.

A génoise can be made several days before it is needed. It keeps very well in a metal or plastic container in the refrigerator. If you like, you can add a touch of vanilla or any other kind of flavoring before baking it in a low to moderate oven.

To test whether the génoise is done, insert the point of a knife into the middle; it should be clean when pulled out.

3. The mixture should be very light and creamy. If other flavors are desired, add them now.

4. Precisely butter and flour a cake pan, tapping off any excess flour. Pour half of the batter into the pan, making sure it is evenly distributed.

Chocolate Génoise

5. Butter and flour a second pan. Thoroughly blend the cocoa powder into the remaining batter and pour it into the second pan. Bake both génoise for 20 minutes in a low-to-moderate oven.

6. When the génoise are finished, turn them out of the cake pans. Leave them upside-down until they have cooled into an even shape.

Buttercream

1. *Pour the water into a saucepan. Add the sugar and cook over medium heat. As the syrup thickens, remove the crystals forming around the sides of the pan with a pastry brush dipped in water.*

Ingredients:
6½ tbsp/100 ml water
½ cup/125 g sugar
5 egg yolks
1 cup/250 g butter
vanilla extract

Preparation time: 30 minutes
Cooking time: 10 minutes
Difficulty: ✶✶

2. *Whisk the egg yolks, passing the bowl over the stove burner from time to time to keep them just warm. When the sugar syrup has become sticky, but before it starts to darken, pour it slowly onto the egg yolks, whisking vigorously all the time.*

As you may know, buttercream plays an important role in the creation of many kinds of gâteau. It is also used for decoration and fillings. It derives its light and delicate consistency from the cooked sugar, or sugar syrup, it contains, which also helps it stay fresh longer.

If you follow our chef's hints, you will be able to produce a perfect buttercream.

Pay close attention to the syrup while cooking: This is the trickiest stage and the final results depend on it.

The syrup is ready to pour slowly over the beaten egg yolks when the syrup forms ribbons when dropped from the spoon. Don't neglect to whisk the yolks vigorously during the whole of this operation, and continue until the mixture has cooled completely. At this point you can add the butter.

If the buttercream has been stored in the refrigerator until needed, beat it at room temperature for a few moments before using.

Buttercream can be flavored with coffee, chocolate, orange liqueur, or other flavors.

3. *When the syrup and yolks are thoroughly blended, continue whisking until the mixture is completely cooled; it should be very frothy. Gradually add the softened butter. Flavor with a little vanilla extract or other flavoring, and refrigerate until needed.*

Pastry Cream

Ingredients:
½ cup plus 2 tbsp/150 g
   superfine sugar
6 egg yolks
½ cup plus 2 tbsp/75 g flour
vanilla extract
2 cups/500 ml milk

Preparation time: 10 minutes
Cooking time: 5 minutes
Difficulty: ✶✶

1. Add the sugar to the egg yolks and stir together briskly for 1 minute. Gradually sift in the flour while stirring vigorously to prevent lumps from forming. Add the vanilla extract (or other flavoring).

2. Bring the milk to a boil in a saucepan, then gradually pour it onto the egg yolks, stirring very gently.

Pastry cream, or *crème pâtissière*, is used as the basis of many sweet dishes and pastries. While the cream is cooking, you must watch very carefully to ensure that it does not boil. As soon as you feel it beginning to thicken, remove it from the heat, but continue whisking briskly for a few moments. Transfer the thickening pastry cream immediately to another receptacle to stop the cooking process.

Add whatever flavoring you have chosen just before you are going to use the cream.

In the majority of cases, pastry cream appears alone, especially as the cold filling for tarts, choux pastry puffs and other pastries. However, it can also be used hot, or it can be combined with whipped cream or buttercream for a lighter, richer filling.

Pastry chefs make great use of this versatile cream when creating their most sumptuous, mouthwatering gâteaux. Enjoy creating your own special effects with crème pâtissière!

3. When the milk is thoroughly blended in, transfer the mixture to the saucepan. Heat it while stirring continuously. As soon as the surface begins to bubble, remove the cream from the heat and transfer to a cool bowl. Whisk again for a few moments.

Short Pastry

1. Sift the flour onto a smooth work surface in a mound. Make a well in the center and break the egg into it. Mix these 2 ingredients.

Ingredients:
2 cups/250 g flour
1 egg
10 tbsp/150 g butter
4 tsp/20 g sugar
¼ tsp salt
water

Preparation time: 10 minutes
Resting time: 40 minutes
Difficulty: ✶

2. Add the butter, sugar, and salt. Begin kneading the dough and add a little water at a time until it just forms a smooth paste.

Short pastry is the most commonly used pastry for pie crusts and tart shells, whether the filling be savory or sweet, and is very easy to prepare. This particular recipe is unusual in that it includes an egg, making the pastry a bit richer.

In French there are two terms for short pastry: *pâte brisée* (the recipe given here) is used for a pie or tart. When the pastry is used for a turnover or dumpling, the sugar is omitted and it becomes *pâte à foncer*. Also, for savory recipes, use oil instead of butter and add less water. Sweet short pastry, or *pâte sucrée*, is a short pastry with additional sugar (2 tbsp) added to the dry flour.

Short pastry can be prepared the day before it will be used. Wrap it in a dish towel and keep it in the refrigerator. Remove the pastry 15 minutes before rolling it out.

Whichever version you require, be sure to use just enough water so that the dough is neither too moist nor too dry.

Short pastry is very easy to use and is not fragile.

3. When the pastry is smooth and well-kneaded, flatten it with the palm of your hand. Let it sit 30–40 minutes before using.

Almond Biscuit

1. Stir together the ground almonds and sugar, then add the sifted flour. Beat in the unbeaten egg yolks.

Ingredients:
- 1¼ cups/225 g ground almonds
- ¾ cup plus 3 tbsp/225 g superfine sugar
- ½ cup/60 g flour, sifted
- 3 egg yolks
- 6 tbsp/90 g butter
- 6 egg whites
- a pinch of salt

Preparation time: 10 minutes
Cooking time: 20 minutes
Difficulty: ✷✷

2. Melt the butter and add it while whisking very vigorously. Begin whipping the egg whites, add a pinch of salt, and continue whipping until they form very stiff peaks. Fold them gently into the almond mixture.

Like a classic sponge cake, most variations of biscuit not only contain whipped egg whites, but are in fact leavened by them, which has the effect of making the final result lighter. There are almost infinite variations of biscuit to be discovered in French recipes.

This recipes differs slightly from a classic sponge cake, in which the superfine sugar and egg yolks are beaten in a mixing bowl to the ribbon stage before the flour and/or ground nuts and then finally the egg whites are folded in. For this almond biscuit, the ground nuts, sugar and sifted flour are combined before the egg yolks are beaten in.

If desired, several drops of orange-flower water can be added with the beaten egg whites. The biscuit must be baked in an oven preheated to 355 °F/180 °C. When done, you can either use the cake as a base for a gâteau, or simply spread the almond sponge with apricot jam, pastry cream, or another type of preserves or filling. This almond biscuit can be used in the preparation of a wide range of desserts.

3. Pour the batter onto a baking sheet covered with buttered parchment paper and bake at 355 °F/180 °C for about 20 minutes. If you wish, decorate the biscuit with melted chocolate in a small paper cone.

Chocolate Sauce

Ingredients:
- 8¾ oz/250 g baking chocolate
- 2 tbsp milk
- 3½ tbsp/50 g softened butter
- 1⅓ cups/200 g confectioners' sugar
- 6½ tbsp/100 ml heavy cream
- 2 egg yolks

Preparation time: 5 minutes
Cooking time: 10 minutes
Difficulty: ✶

1. Place a saucepan in a bain-marie. Break the chocolate into small pieces and melt slowly. Pour in the milk. Add the butter and stir gently.

2. Sift the confectioners' sugar onto the melted chocolate. Pour in the cream, and again stir gently.

This delicious chocolate sauce can be served either hot or cold. If it is to be served warm, prepare the sauce at the last moment. It is very quick and easy to make and can be used to accompany many types of desserts, or as a coating for a gâteau.

The chef recommends melting the chocolate in a bain-marie; otherwise use a saucepan with a heavy bottom. In any case, the heat must be kept very low.

After you have added the softened butter and heavy cream to the melted chocolate, stir the sauce with a wooden spoon to obtain a completely smooth mixture.

Always use a wooden spoon when stirring in confectioners' sugar and eggs. You must work very quickly when stirring in the egg yolks, because they must not be allowed to coagulate. If you like, flavor your sauce with coffee, substituting strong coffee for milk; or add 2 tsp rum, Cognac or whisky at the end of cooking. However, choose carefully, because not all flavors blend well with chocolate.

3. Add the yolks to the chocolate sauce, blend them in thoroughly, and serve.

Fond de Succès

Ingredients:
- 3½ tbsp/50 g superfine sugar
- 4½ tbsp/50 g ground almonds
- 4 tsp/10 g flour, sifted
- ⅓ oz/10 g powdered milk, sifted
- 5 egg whites
- 6½ tbsp/100 g sugar (for whisking the egg whites)

1. Combine the superfine sugar and ground almonds. Stir in the flour, then the powdered milk. Whisk the egg whites into stiff peaks, gradually adding the sugar.

Preparation time: 20 minutes
Cooking time: 15 minutes
Difficulty: ✶✶✶

2. Gently fold the egg whites into the almond mixture.

A *fond de succès* is a cake made from an almond meringue mixture. It can be served on its own, or made into something extraordinary by filling and frosting it with praline cream. Traditionally, the fond is cut into small squares on which the letter "S" is written in royal icing, but it can also be filled with buttercream or pastry cream and made into petits fours. The blanched almonds must first be crushed and then ground into a powder.

The egg whites must be whisked into very stiff peaks before being gently folded into the almond and sugar dry mixture. Pour the meringue mixture into a flan ring placed on a buttered and floured baking sheet, filling it to a depth of about 2 in/5 cm.

Bake at 355 °F/180 °C for 10-15 minutes. When it is done, remove the flan ring and leave the fond de succès to cool on the baking sheet.

3. Grease and flour a baking sheet. With the aid of either a flan ring or a pastry bag, form large discs of the fond de succès mixture. Bake at 355 °F/180 °C for about 15 minutes.

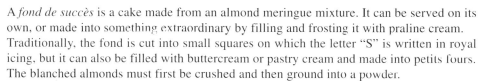

Choux Pastry

Ingredients:
⅔ cup/160 g butter
2 cups/500 ml water
pinch salt
2 generous cups/250 g
 flour, sifted
1 tbsp/15 g superfine sugar
5 eggs

1. Melt the butter in a saucepan containing the water and a pinch of salt. Add the flour and sugar and stir together thoroughly.

Preparation time: 20 minutes
Cooking time: 20 minutes
Difficulty: ✷✷

2. Heat the dough gently, stirring continuously until it dries out some and comes away from the sides of the pan.

Pâte à choux, or choux pastry, was once known in French as *pâte à chaud*, or hot pastry. It is unique in that it is cooked twice, first on the stove, and then in the oven.

It can be used in a wide range of recipes, both sweet and savory; in that case you should omit the sugar.

Measure your ingredients very accurately. It is essential to mix the water, butter, salt, sugar and flour together very thoroughly.

Watch the dough while stirring it over the heat: When it comes away cleanly from the side of the pan, this means all the water has evaporated.

Add the eggs whole, one at a time. Be careful not to let the eggs coagulate because of the mixture being too hot.

Form small choux pastry puffs using a pastry bag and nozzle. Brush them with beaten egg and bake in a hot oven, starting at 400 °F/200 °C then lowering to 350 °F/180 °C to finish baking. Do not on any account open the oven door while the choux pastry puffs are baking!

3. Remove from the heat add beat the eggs in, one by one. Using a pastry bag and nozzle, form small pastry puffs on a greased baking sheet and bake in a moderately hot oven.

Sablée Pastry

Ingredients:
1½ cups plus 2 tbsp/
    200 g flour
2 eggs
¼ tsp salt
½ cup/120 g sugar
½ cup/120 g butter

1. Sift the flour into a bowl. Stir in the eggs and salt. Add the sugar and mix together.

Preparation time: 15 minutes
Resting time: 2–3 hours
Difficulty: ✶ ✶

2. Cream the butter in a separate bowl, then blend it in and begin to knead the dough, incorporating a little more flour until the pastry comes away cleanly from the sides of the bowl.

There is a slight difference between a sablée pastry and a sweet short pastry. *Pâte sablée* is aerated, richer in eggs and butter and therefore more crumbly, while *pâte brisée sucrée*, or sweet short pastry, is drier and firmer. Sablée pastry is richer and finer in texture, and is ideal for making tarts and other types of *pâtisserie*.

The flour, eggs, sugar and salt must be stirred together with a light and delicate touch. Cream the butter until it is light and fluffy before adding it to the mixture.

Blend it in thoroughly and start to knead the dough. To obtain a truly smooth dough, the French like to flatten it with the heel of the hand a few times.

Form the dough into a ball, cover it with a cloth, and set it aside in a cool place to become firmer before using it, for example, to line a tart form. If possible, prepare the dough the day before it will be needed.

3. Place the pastry on a floured work surface and flatten it with the heel of the hand to remove any lumps. Return it to the bowl and allow it to rest, covered, for 2–3 hours before using.

Crêpe Batter

Ingredients:
- 2 generous cups/250 g flour
- 2 tbsp butter
- a pinch of salt
- 6 eggs
- 6½ tbsp/100 g superfine sugar
- 3 cups/750 ml milk
- zest of 1 lime
- 3½ tbsp/50 ml aged rum

1. Sift the flour into a large bowl. Melt the butter, cool slightly, and stir it in with a pinch of salt. Break in the eggs, then add the sugar.

Preparation time: 15 minutes
Resting time: 1 hour
Difficulty: ✶✶

Crêpes are deceptively simple. While they require nothing particularly difficult or fancy, some care is needed in preparing perfect crêpes.

Cook them in a heavy-bottomed pan so that they do not stick.

Let the batter rest for about an hour before actually making the crêpes; in fact, it will keep for one or two days in the refrigerator.

Crêpes are incredibly versatile, and can be used as the basis for a variety of recipes. If you want to prepare a dish based on savory crêpes, omit the lime zest and sugar from this recipe. Crêpes are suitable for serving at any time of day. Whatever way you choose to prepare them, they will always be greeted with enthusiasm.

2. Stir these ingredients until the batter is smooth and free of lumps. Pour in the milk, stirring vigorously. Add the lime zest and the rum. Mix well with a whisk. Let the batter rest at least 1 hour before making the crêpes.

3. Lightly butter a frying pan, but only for the first few crêpes. Make the crêpes as thin as possible.

Puff Pastry

Ingredients:
2½ lbs/1.3 kg cake flour
4 generous cups/1 kg butter
2 tbsp/35 g salt
2 cups/500 ml ice-cold water
flour for the work surface

1. Blend 2½ cups/300 g flour into all but 6½ tbsp/100 g of the butter and refrigerate. Mound the remaining flour, make a well in its center and place the salt, reserved butter, and a little ice-cold water in it. Begin to knead with the fingertips, adding just enough water to yield a pliable paste. Refrigerate for 30 minutes.

Preparation time: 1 hour 30 minutes
Cooking time: 20 minutes
Chilling time: 2 hours
Difficulty ✳ ✳ ✳

2. Working quickly, roll the dough into a wide rectangle. Place the butter and flour mixture in its center. Fold the pastry over the butter mixture. Carefully, again roll out the pastry into a long rectangular strip. Fold in thirds with the ends overlapping in the middle. This is 1 "turn" of the dough. Repeat the process 2 more times.

The ideal surface for making puff pastry is a marble countertop or cutting board, especially in the summer months when the pastry must be kept as cold as possible.

Though puff pastry can be temperamental and requires a certain touch, if you follow these directions closely, your pastry is sure to be a success.

The dough must be made quickly and kneaded firmly, yet with a light touch to retain the air pockets that give puff pastry its characteristic layers. Keep the pastry as cold as possible, and work it with your fingertips.

When all the flour has been incorporated, form the dough into a ball and make a few cuts in it to allow air to circulate. Refrigerate in between steps.

When you have created your masterpiece, brush the outer layer of pastry with beaten egg before baking to give it a golden sheen.

3. Refrigerate the dough for 1 hour. Remove it and perform 4 more turns. Refrigerate again, and finish with 6 additional turns. The pastry is now ready to be used in any way you like.

Glossary

APRICOT GLAZE: Hot, strained apricot jam can be spread onto pastries, either as a glaze or as an isolating layer between cake and moist cream or fruit fillings.

BAIN-MARIE: A gentle method of heating used to either cook food or keep cooked food warm, a bain-marie consists of a pan containing food placed inside a larger pan of warm (not boiling) water, surrounding the smaller pan with heat. Placed in an oven, a bain-marie generates steam for foods that require moister heat than that generated by home ovens.

BANYULS: A sweet fortified wine made in a place in southwestern France of the same name. Port would be an acceptable substitute if Banyuls is not available.

BAVAROIS: French for Bavarian cream, a chilled dessert based on a mixture of custard, crème chantilly and gelatin.

BISCUIT: The French word for sponge cake.

TO BLANCH: Briefly immersing foods in boiling water and then in cold water to stop the cooking. This process makes it easier to remove peels and skins, rids food of impurities, and preserves the flavor and color of food before freezing.

BRIOCHE: A classic French yeast bread, very light, yet made very rich by eggs and butter.

CARAMEL: Caramel is produced when sugar is heated to 320-350 °F/160-177 °C and becomes light to dark brown. Other ingredients like water, cream and butter are added to the caramel to make sauces or candies, but liquid must be added carefully and gradually to sugar heated to these temperatures!

TO CARAMELIZE: To heat sugar until it becomes caramel; or to coat something with caramel syrup; or to sprinkle sugar on the surface of a dessert and then broil or grill it briefly until the sugar turns into caramel (for example, a crème brûlée).

CHANTILLY: A term from French culinary vocabulary, *à la chantilly* means that a dish, sweet or savory, is served with or incorporates whipped cream. Crème chantilly is simply whipped cream, most often lightly sweetened with vanilla, sugar or liqueurs.

CHOUX PASTRY: A simple but unique dough that is prepared on the stovetop by bringing water or milk to a boil, adding flour and then beating in several eggs to form a sticky paste. This is the classic cream puff pastry.

CLARIFIED BUTTER: Butter that has been melted slowly without stirring, then skimmed and decanted, leaving the milk solids and water in the pan. This liquid is pure butter fat and has a higher smoking point than whole butter, but less intense flavor.

TO CLARIFY: To remove any particles which interfere with the clear appearance of liquids (i.e. jelly or consommé), usually by straining or binding the impurities, often by adding and then straining out egg white.

TO COAT: In baking, coating refers to covering the surface of cakes and pastries with a thin layer often of chocolate or marzipan.

CONFECTIONERS' SUGAR: American term for icing sugar, also known as powdered sugar.

COULIS: A thick sauce consisting primarily of puréed fruit, occasionally with lemon juice or sugar added.

CRÈME FRAÎCHE: A thickened cream with an incomparably smooth texture and nutty, not sour, taste. It is indispensable in French cuisine, particularly in sauces since it does not separate when boiled. If not readily available, crème fraîche can be simulated by adding 1 tsp–1 tbsp buttermilk to 1 cup heavy cream and letting the mixture stand at room temperature 8–24 hours until thickened. This will keep up to 10 days in the refrigerator.

TO DEGLAZE: To use a liquid such as water, alcohol or stock to dissolve food particles in a pan after food has been sautéed in it. This liquid is normally used as the basis of a sauce.

TO DICE: To cut fruit or vegetables into even, dice-like shapes. Traditionally, dice is about ¼–½ in/5 mm in size.

DOUBLE BOILER: A double boiler consists of two pans that nestle into each other. The bottom pan is filled with simmering water and the top pan rests over, but not in, the hot water, providing the gentle heat necessary to melt or cook delicate foods like custards or sauces. Compare to bain-marie.

TO FLAMBÉ: To pour alcohol over food and light the alcohol, imparting a very special flavor. This can be a dramatic presentation or an earlier step in the cooking process.

TO FLOUR: Also called dusting, this means coating a greased baking pan with a very fine layer of flour so that the item baked in it can be more easily removed. Other ingredients can be used instead of flour including, for example, sugar, bread crumbs, sesame seeds, or finely ground almonds.

TO FOLD: Also to blend; a means of combining two mixtures of varying densities (for example, egg whites and custard). With the lighter mass on top of the heavier one, use a spatula to cut through both, scrape along the bottom of the bowl, and up the side. Continue this, rotating the bowl slightly with each stroke. Folding must be done carefully, gently, and yet rapidly to retain the volume of the lighter mixture.

GANACHE: An extraordinary, rich chocolate cream made by heating whipping cream and allowing chocolate to melt in it. Depending on its texture, it can be used as a coating, filling, or sauce.

TO GARNISH: Decorating a dish to make it more visually appealing with various edible elements; also refers to the decoration itself. Garnish varies from a single sprig of mint, to the additions to a soup, to entire dishes served with the main entrée.

GELATIN: A clear and flavorless substance used to jell liquid mixtures. Gelatin is available in ¼ oz/7 g envelopes of granules (more common in North America) and in paper-thin sheets or leaves (standard in Europe). Leaf gelatin should be soaked in cold water for 5–10 minutes, then thoroughly wrung out before, like ground gelatin, being dissolved in a small amount of hot liquid before use. One needs 1 envelope or 4 leaves of gelatin to jell 2 cups/500 ml liquid.

GÉNOISE: A close relative of the sponge cake, in which whole eggs are beaten with sugar to the ribbon stage before flour, finely-ground nuts or other ingredients are folded in.

GLACÉ: A French term meaning chilled, iced or frozen.

TO GLAZE: To spread a thin layer of eggs, jelly or jam, gum arabic, or any other kind of coating onto foods to give them a shiny finish.

TO GREASE: Brushing a thin layer of butter or some other fat onto baking pans so that the finished product can be removed from the pans without tearing.

HEAVY CREAM: This is the American term for double cream.

HOT OVEN: 400–425 °F or 205–220 °C

TO INFUSE: see to steep

ITALIAN MERINGUE: A variation of meringue made by pouring hot sugar syrup over whipped egg whites while beating continuously until the mixture has cooled completely.

TO KNEAD: To thoroughly combine and work the components of a dough either by hand or with the dough hook of an electric mixer to produce a homogenous dough. It can take 15 minutes or longer to produce a smooth, elastic dough when kneading by hand.

LIGHT CREAM: This is the American term for single cream.

TO LINE: To cover the inside of a mold or pan with whatever ingredient is called for. For a charlotte, ladyfingers would be used. For aspic, the mold would be lined with gelatin.

LOW OVEN: 300–325 °F or 150–165 °C

TO MACERATE/MARINATE: To soak foods in an aromatic liquid (marinade) for a period of time to allow the food to take on the flavor of the liquid and become more tender. Fruits soaked in liqueur are macerated; meat or fish in a savory liquid is marinated.

MELON BALLER: A special spoon shaped like a tiny bowl used to carve circles from melons and other fruits and vegetables.

MERINGUE: A light mass of stiffly beaten egg whites, usually sweetened with a little sugar, which can be used as an icing or topping, an element of a mousse, cream or soufflé, or baked as cookies or bases for gâteau. See also Italian meringue.

MILLEFEUILLE: The French word literally means "thousand leaves" and refers to the many buttery-light layers of perfect puff pastry. Millefeuille is also a 3-tiered sweet consisting of puff pastry filled with cream, custard or fruit and dusted with confectioners' sugar or glazed on top. The classic version, with pastry cream, is known as a Napoleon in North America, or vanilla slice in Britain.

MODERATE OVEN: 350–375 °F or 175–190 °C

PÂTE: The French word for many kinds of mixtures in baking, including dough, batter and pastry. Short pastry is *pâte brisée*, short sweet pastry is *pâte sucrée*, crêpe batter is *pâte à crêpe*, and so forth.

PINEAU: A sweet, fortified white wine made in the Cognac region of France. If this is unavailable, a mixture of grape juice and cognac may be substituted.

TO POACH: A method of cooking food by immersing it in hot, but not boiling, water or other liquid.

TO PREBAKE: To bake a pie crust or pastry shell without a filling. Prick the pastry with fork and weight it down with dried beans or baking beans so it does not rise or contort while baking.

TO PURÉE: To blend or mash food until it has a perfectly smooth consistency, often by means of a blender or food processor. Purée also refers to the puréed food itself.

TO RECONSTITUTE: To add liquid to dried or dehydrated foods, such as powdered milk or dried fruits and vegetables.

TO REDUCE: The fundamental step in sauce preparation is to cook a mixture until some of the liquid has evaporated, resulting in a thicker and more intensely-flavored sauce.

TO REFRESH: A means of preventing foods from continuing to cook in their own heat either by immersing the cooking pan in cold water or running cold water directly onto the food immediately after removing it from the heat.

RIBBON STAGE: When beating sugar with eggs, they should reach the ribbon stage, so called because the mixture falls in silky ribbons from the whisk or beaters.

SABAYON: Also known by its Italian name, zabaglione, it is an extremely light, frothy custard consisting of egg yolks, sugar and wine or other spirits that are vigorously whisked over a gentle source of heat.

TO SAUTÉ: A method of cooking in a very small amount of hot oil or other fat, usually in an uncovered pan. Food may be lightly sautéed just to brown its surface, or cooked all the way through.

SPONGE CAKE: A classic sponge cake consists of egg whites and egg yolks, each beaten separately with sugar until light and foamy, then folded together and enriched with a little flour, ground nuts, or other ingredients. There are virtually infinite variations of sponge cakes, and they form the basis of a vast array of gâteaus and other desserts.

TO STEEP OR INFUSE: To soak an ingredient in a liquid, usually hot, for several minutes in order to impart its flavor to the liquid (for example, tea in hot water, or a vanilla bean in milk when making custard).

TO STRAIN: To pour or press ingredients through a sieve or a piece of cheesecloth in order to remove impurities, lumps, or seeds.

SUGAR SYRUP: A solution of sugar and water that have been boiled together. It is indispensable in baking and confection-making. The density of sugar syrup varies according to the proportions of sugar and water used; unless otherwise noted the recipes in this volume call for a heavy syrup made of equal parts sugar and water.

VANILLA SUGAR: Sugar infused with the flavor of vanilla bean, or containing some ground vanilla. This can easily be made at home by placing one or more vanilla beans in a jar filled with sugar. After a week or two the sugar will be permeated with the aroma of vanilla.

VERY HOT OVEN: 450–475 °F or 230–245 °C

The Participating Chefs

Lionel Accolas
Chef de Cuisine

Nicolas Albano
Maître Cuisinier de France

Marcel Benoit
Chef de Cuisine

Michel Bignon

Aimé Bizé

Luce Bodinaud

Jean-Claude Bon
Maître Cuisinier de France

Jean Bordier
Maître Cuisinier de France
Meilleur Ouvrier de France

Michel Boureaud
Maître Artisan Pâtissier

Jacques Chibois
Chef des Cuisines

Marc Daniel
Chef de Cuisine

Francis Delage
Chevalier de l'Ordre national du Mérite

Ginette Delaive
Commandeur des Cordon-Bleus de France

Joseph Delphin
Maître Cuisinier de France

Francis Dulucq
Maître Cuisinier de France

Daniel Dumesnil
Chef de Cuisine
Chevalier du Mérite Agricole

Robert Dupuy

Maxime Durand
Chef Pâtissier
Meilleur Ouvrier Glacier de France
Champion de France des Desserts

Roland Durand
Maître Cuisinier de France
Meilleur Ouvrier de France

Odile Engel

Jean-François Ferrié

Charles Floccia
Grand Prix du Dessert du Cedus

Roland Gauthier

Pierre-Jean and Jany Gleize
Maîtres Cuisiniers de France

Charles and Philippe Godard
Maîtres Cuisiniers de France

Lionel Goyard
Chef de Cuisine

Bernard Hémery

Bernard Huguet
Pâtissier-Glacier-Chocolatier
Meilleur Ouvrier Glacier de France

Jean-Pierre Lallement
Maître Cuisinier de France

Serge de La Rochelle

Jean-Michel Lebon

Jean Lenoir
Maître Cuisinier de France
Finaliste Meilleur Ouvrier de France

Bernard Mariller
Chef de Cuisine

Manuel Martinez
Chef de Cuisine
Maître Cuisinier de France
Meilleur Ouvrier de France

Paul-Louis and Michel Meissonnier
Maîtres Cuisiniers de France

Christian Métreau
Chef de Cuisine

Daniel Nachon
Chevalier de l'Ordre du Mérite

Jean-Luis Niqueux
Chef de Cuisine

Alain Nonnet
Chef de Cuisine
Maître Cuisinier de France
Finaliste Meilleur Ouvrier de France

Angelo Orilieri
Chevalier du Mérite Agricole

Claude Patry
Chef de Cuisine

Christian Ravinel
Chef de Cuisine

Claude Ribardière

Armand Roth
Chef de Cuisine

Roger Roucou
Président, Maîtres Cuisiniers de France

Gérard Royant
Maître Cuisinier de France

Georges-Victor Schmitt
Chevalier du Mérite Agricole

Pierre Sébilleau
Chef de Cuisine

Philippe Segond
Meilleur Ouvrier de France

Dominique Toulousy
Maître Cuisinier de France

Gilles Tournadre

Jean Vettard
Maître Cuisinier de France

Huguette Zarka
Commandeur de la Confrérie des Cordons-Bleus

Index of Recipes